About the author

For 40 years Robin Crichton ɪ
Film Studios and was one
leading film producer/directo
particularly in the internation
of films for cinema and ᴛᴠ
Scottish Chairman and ᴜᴋ Vice Chairman
of the Independent Programme Producers
Association and latterly as coproduction
project leader for the Council of Europe.

He studied social anthropology at Paris
and Edinburgh Universities, undertaking fieldwork amongst
American Indians and in a mountain village in Anatolia. At
Edinburgh, he met and married his first wife Trish while
she was doing an honours degree in archaeology. Political
problems between Pakistan and China in the Hindu Kush
led to the abandonment of their joint ᴘʜᴅ and a change of
career into filmmaking.

Widowed and retired, he is now remarried to Flora
Maxwell Stuart and they divide their time between Traquair
in the Scottish Borders and Bélesta la Frontière in the
Pyrénées Orientales where he is Président of the Charles
Rennie Mackintosh Association.

He is author of over 100 film scripts and his previous
books include:

Who Is Santa Claus? – the story behind the legend.
  Canongate 1987.

Silent Mouse – the story behind the writing of Silent Night.
  Ladybird 1990.

Sara – (bilingual French and English with Brigittte Aymard)
  – a story of a missing child and gypsies in the Camargue.
  Hachette 1996.

Monsieur Mackintosh – (bilingual French and English)
  – C.R. Mackintosh's life as a painter in the Pyrénées
  Orientales 1923–27. Luath Press 2006.

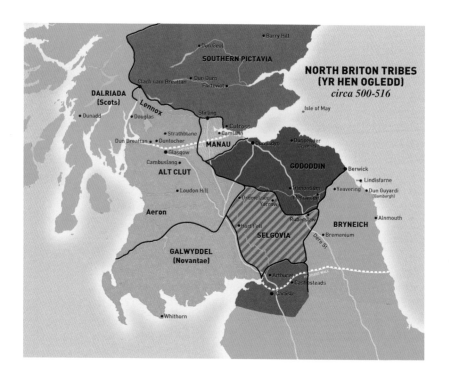

ON THE TRAIL OF
KING ARTHUR

A Journey into Dark Age Scotland
including illustrations maps and itineraries

Written and Photographed by
Robin Crichton

Luath Press Limited
EDINBURGH
www.luath.co.uk

First published 2013

ISBN: 978-1-908373-15-1

The paper used in this book is recyclable. It is made from low
chlorine pulps produced in a low energy, low emissions manner
from renewable forests.

Printed and bound by
Bell & Bain Ltd., Glasgow

Typeset in 9.5 point Sabon by
3btype.com

In memory of Trish,
an archaeologist of considerable talent who
abandoned a promising academic career to share
a life of adventure which led us to discover
lesser-known cultures and places and the riches
of remarkable friendships

'Wherever men are fighting against barbarism, tyranny, and massacre, for freedom, law, and honour, let them remember that the fame of their deeds, even though they themselves be exterminated, may perhaps be celebrated as long as the world rolls round'.

WINSTON CHURCHILL

Contents

List of Illustrations   9
Introduction   13

Arthur of the Britons   18
The Roman Legacy   25
Post Roman Britain 410–490AD   33
The Arthurian Campaign 490–516 AD   56
    The First Five Battles A Defensive Campaign?   58
    The Sixth Battle A Fight For The Crown?   68
    The Seventh and Eighth Battles An Offensive?   72
    The Ninth Battle An Alliance against the Angles? 87
    The Tenth and Eleventh Battles Angles or Picts?   91
    The Twelfth Battle The defeat of the Saxon   96
The Arthurian Peace 516–537AD   104
Merlin – The Druid Versus the Saint   125
The Last of 'The Men of the North'   135
Conclusion   138
The Development of The Legend   141

Timeline   149
Appendix 1 – The Roman Occupation   153
Gazeteer   163
Looking For Arthur   164
The Arthur Trail – The Trail in 12 Days   165
    North Northumberland Hadrian's Wall   166
    North Northumberland Bryneich   168
    Scottish Borders, East Lothian and Midlothian
      Selgovae and Gododdin   169
    West Lothian and Stirlingshire
      The Antonine Wall   172
    Stirling, Clackmannan and East Fife
      The Manau Gododdin   173
    Angus, Perthshire and Lennox The Picts   174
    Argyle The Scots   177

Dumbarton Alt Clut 179
Upper Tweeddale and Dumfries Merlin 180
Galloway St Ninian 182
Ayrshire Aeron 183
England York 184
Bath Little Solsbury Hill 185
Dorset Badbury Rings 186

To Follow the Legend 187
Bibliography 188
Acknowledgements 189

List of Illustrations

Etchings

From *Idylls of the King by Gustav Doré*
  pages 13, 14, 59, 62, 97, 113, 115, 123,
  124, 132, 140, 144, 145, 148

Maps

North Briton Tribes c.500–516	2
Yr Hen Ogledd	
Britain c.400 AD	28
Cunedda's Invasion Of Wales	37
Britain c.516 AD	
Arno Vilanove	103
Britain c.630 AD	
Arno Vilanove	137
Henry II Norman Kingdom	142
Roman Campaigns in North	
Britain 80–84 AD	153
Roman Britannia c.150 AD	160

Photographs

Kirriemuir Stone	16
Four Horsemen	
Meigle Museum	20
A cow with a bell	
Pictavia	21
A hunter with shield and spear at Eassie Churchyard, Angus	22
A hunter on horseback with a hound chasing wild boar	
Pictavia	22
Reconstruction of a Celtic Homestead at Rochester, Northumberland	23
An abandoned Celtic homestead at Rochester, Northumberland	24
Hadrian's Wall Reconstruction at Vindolanda	25
Model of Roman Fort at Vindolanda	26
The base of Hadrian's Wall at Steel Rig just above Vindolanda	27
Photograph by Alexander Curle of the	

Horde at the time of the discovery in 1920	29
Antonine Wall at Watling Lodge	30
Roman cavalry saddle	32
The Mannan Stone now in Clackmannan, but originally a standing stone which stood near the shore on the Manau/Pictish boundary and is believed to havebeen dedicated to a sea god	35
Dere Street still runs from Edinburgh	36
St Ninian's Cave Isle of Whithorn	40
Foundations of St Ninian's church Whithorn	40
Candida Casa, Isle of Whithorn	40
Ruins of the medieval Whithorn Priory	41
Dun Breatan today (top) and as it might have appeared c.500 (bottom) – capital of Alt Clut'.	
Tandem	42
Dumbarton Rock from the west	43
Dunpender (Traprain) Law – a circular structure	45
Dunpender (Traprain Law), the Gododdin Capital from the west	45
Dunpender (Traprain) Law – the water reservoir	45
Base of stone rampart	46
Dun Eidyn (Edinburgh Castle)	46
Dun Guyardi (Bamburgh Castle)	47
Dunadd – capital of the Scots and scene of early coronations with the Stone of Destiny	48
Ritual footsteps and font in the rocks near the Dunadd summit	49
View to the bay where the ships arrived from Ireland	49
The entrance from below and within the fort	50

Dunadd Above: The stone base of the ramparts 50

The well 51

Cavalry attacking spearmen
Pictavia 51

Lindisfarne 53

Horseman Meigle Museum 57

Scots Pines 57

Possible site of the First Battle beside the Glen Water in Ayrshire 60

7th century monastic bell at Fortingall 61

Clach nam Breatan 61

Alt Fionn Ghleann (the line of trees mark the river) 61

Falls of Falloch the Briton/Pictish border 63

The North end of Loch Lomond 63

River Glen Northumberland 64

Holy Island – site of the Angle settlement 64

Glen Falloch 65

The river Dubh Eas 65

Glen Douglas 66

Dunadd as it might have appeared in the 7th century
Peter Dennis, Osprey Publishing 67

River Clyde (Clut) at Cambuslang 69

The Aln just above Bassington 71

Alnmouth 72

Dundurn Hill Fort today and as it might have been in the 6th century 73

An impression of Dundurn in the 6th century
Peter Dennis, Osprey Publishing 74

Pictavia 76

A Traquair Bear – a folk memory of Selgovian times? 76

The Yarrow Valley 77

The Yarrow Stone with its faint inscription 78

The Glebe Stone 78

Warriors Rest 78

Yarrow Water running through an area of natural forest 78

The Catrail in the Cheviots marked by a V in the burnside and a line of dark green marsh grass 79

The Vallum behind Hadrian's Wall 80

Dun Geal sits on top of the whitish rock face 82

Dun Gael – the stone base of the ramparts 82

Dun Gael – rampart base at the entrance 82

The Fortingall community and church as it may have looked
Fortingall Community Council 83

The Nine Maidens Well at Inchadney 84

Whitehill Fort with circular rampart and Ruberslaw on the summit behind 85

Gala Water 85

St Mary's Well near Stowe 86

Remains of the Roman city wall of York (Ebrauc) 88

The site of the Roman ferry crossing of Dere Street to Petravia 89

The Humber at the site of the ferry crossing 90

A Pictish warship
Paul Wagner, Osprey Publishing 92

Terracing on Arthurs Seat 94

Arthurs Seat 95

Remains of the Main Gate
Bremenium 96

Badbury Rings from the east 98

The North Entrance through the ramparts and ditch 99

The Inner Rampart – the two figures show the scale. On top of the base was a wooden pallisade 99

Solsbury Hill 101

Stirling – Castle Rock, the capital of Manau 104

Abbey Craig 105

Base of the Abbey Craig rampart 105

Castle Rock from Abbey Craig 106

Camelon in the 19th century
Falkirk Local History Society 106
The Roman fort of Colonia was sited
on top of the hill at what today is
Falkirk Golf Course 107
View from the site of Camelon Fort
towards the distant Ochils 107
K. Halleswelle 110
Arthur's O'en before demolition 112
Arthur's O'en 18th century replica at
Penicuik House 112
Barry Hill by Alyth 116
Daniel and the lions or Vanora
(Guinevere) being killed by wild
animals? 116
Vanora's Mound Meigle Kirkyard 117
The river Carron – three miles
downriver from Camelon 118
Arthur on the barge to Avalon
Robert Hope 118
The River Forth below Stirling 119
The graveyard at Eccles (St Ninians).
Was this the last resting place of
Arthur? 119
Cambuskenneth Abbey from the river 120
The Solway 121
Engraving on the lead cross in the
tomb in Glastonbury 122
The cliff on Dunpender (Traprain)
Law 126
Low tide on the foreshore at Culross 127
St Serf, Thenau and Mungo 127
Culross Abbey 128
The river Esk 129
The site of the battle on the banks of
the Esk 129
Church commemorating the Christian
victory at Adderyd 129
Hart Fell 130
Merlin's view of the valley below 130
The Cleugh 130
A Rock Shelter 131
Stobo Kirk 132

The Alter Stane 133
Merlin receives communion across the
Powsail Burn 133
Merlin's grave marked by the fenced off
thorn bush on the right 133
Merlindale in the Upper Tweed by
Drumelzier 134
Dun Guyardi (Bamburgh) 135
Holy Island 136
Avallon today and as it was 143
From a stone in Govan Old Parish
Kirk 151
Dunpender (Traprain Law) as it might
have been in 100 AD 154
Crannog 155
Forest – ideal cover for Guerrilla
warfare 155
Ditch of the Antonine Wall near
Twechar 158
Ceremonial helmet from Trimontium 159
Antonine Wall at Twechar 159
Eildon Hills the three mountains of
Trimontium with their important Iron
Age hillfort 159
Crannog Loch Tay 161

Introduction

KING ARTHUR and the Knights of the Round Table is one of the world's great legends. Everyone knows the story:

How, as a boy, Arthur innocently drew a sword from a stone and was proclaimed the rightful king.

How the wizard, Merlin, became his advisor and when Arthur's sword broke, Merlin took him to a lake where an arm bearing a new sword broke the surface and an enchantress, the Lady of the Lake, told him it was called Excalibur. With it, he would vanquish all his foes.

How he was joined at Camelot by the Knights of the Round Table, men of honour who together pursued adventures, rescuing damsels in distress, fighting giants and monsters and making conquests from Iceland to the Alps.

From *Idyllis of the King* – Gustav Doré

How they went in quest of the Holy Grail.

And finally, how Arthur was betrayed by Guinevere which caused his final battle and his death on the Isle of Avalon.

For more than a thousand years, the story of Arthur has been adapted by successive generations to fit the morality and colour of their own age. It is perhaps the longest running soap opera in literary history.

The real Arthur – if there was a real Arthur – lived around the turn of the 6th century, a time of oral rather than written tradition. It was an age when scribes were few and far between, and history was passed on through word of mouth by successive generations of bards. It was often many years after the events had actually taken place that the stories were finally written down. Then, over the centuries, in the process of recopying, those original accounts were embellished and relocated from forgotten to familiar places and made more relevant to the times. In the literary sources

that do survive, Arthur appears essentially as a passing reference.

Old Welsh (Brythonic) was the common language of the whole of Celtic Britain south of the Scottish Highlands. The earliest accounts, which are often in Latin, were written mainly by Welsh speaking clerics and later supplemented by Gaelic speaking Irish writers

The earliest author is a monk named Gildas who was born within the lifetime of Arthur but, as will be revealed, had good reason to resent him. In his account of *The Overthrow and Conquest of Britain,* Gildas is more concerned with writing a moral treatise on the decline and decadence of British society than a strictly factual history.

Another monk, Nennius, is credited with writing his *Historia Brittonum* in about 829/830. But it has been shown that in fact this is not the work of a single author but rather a complex compilation of historical annals and stories which had already been edited and altered by synchronising historians in the 7th and 8th centuries.

There are also various annals written later but probably copied from 6th century texts, two of whose authors (Taliesin and Lllywarch Hen) were quite possibly from Lennox – the northernmost district of Alt Clut (Strathclyde) and the likely terrain of Arthur's early battles. Although the poems are fanciful, they indicate geographical locations and events. But how much is true?

These 'sources' were usually produced, with some

political intent for vested interests. This is particularly true for the Lives of Saints which were written to promote a Christian message. As historical records of events that supposedly took place, often hundreds of years before, other contemporary sources with which they could be cross-checked rarely exist and so they cannot be taken at face value.

The problem for the academic historian is that his conclusions must be based on being able to check and crosscheck reliable documentary sources. History in the Dark Ages was not the academic study which it is today. History was about identity – the ancestors. It was also about ideals of morality and achievement. It was educational in a subjective rather than objective sense, with certain elements emphasised and others skimmed over or forgotten.

As a social anthropologist I did field work with a tribe of North American Indians. Their history was also essentially oral, passed down from generation to generation, especially with regard to earlier times, before the coming of the white man. My tribe believed that they were created first amongst all the tribes of North America. A few years ago DNA tests showed that indeed they had not crossed from Asia into Alaska like most of the other tribes but appear to have originated in Southern France and made their way across the Atlantic following the edge of the retreating Ice Cap. So there can be grains of truth behind a legend.

Arthur's Britain represents a blank spot in existing history books. Above the Highland line, we read of the Scots and the Picts, but very rarely is there any mention of 'The Men of the North' – the Britons who occupied the area north of Hadrian's Wall in what is now southern Scotland. These are perhaps the darkest times in British Dark Age history – the Forgotten Times.

Arthur exists in Celtic lore. He was a Celtic hero. Writers of history are inevitably selective, evaluating events and extolling virtues from their own cultural and political perspective. From an Anglo Saxon point of view, Arthur's crushing defeats were a disaster and best forgotten. Consequently, the Anglo Saxons wrote him out.

Today, Arthur is a subject where modern historians tread

at their academic peril. In 1973, Professor John Morris of University College London published a history of the Dark Ages entitled *The Age of Arthur*. Although he did not find a lot to say about Arthur *per se*, he did acknowledge a possible grain of truth for his existence. The reaction of the academic establishment was almost vitriolic. 'We must reject him from our histories and, above all, from the titles of our books' (Professor Dumville, Aberdeen University). 'No figure on the borderline of history and mythology has wasted more of the historian's time.' (Nowell Myres, Oxford University). 'The historian can yet say nothing of value about him.' (Thomas Charles Edwards, Oxford University) But in the last two decades attitudes have gradually changed. 'All 'history' of this period has to rely on a degree of imaginative speculation as well as rigorous scientific research' (Professor Wendy Davies, University College London).

In the 5th and 6th centuries, all we have are probabilities and possibilities. This book attempts to take the little we know about Arthur and place it alongside the little we know about socio-political events at the time. In putting the two together we can make a case for 'probability'. By incorporating oral tradition, we can further suggest 'possibilities.' What follows is a working hypothesis, the truth of which will only be proved or disproved by archaeological enlightenment. 'Proof beyond all reasonable doubt' is

Kirriemuir Stone
Pictavia

tantalisingly out of reach. We are in the realm of what thinkers of the Scottish Enlightenment termed 'conjectural history'.

Was Arthur his real name or an epithet? If he really existed, where did he live? When did he live? What was the social and political background of his times? What did he achieve? If he was so successful, why did he not found a dynasty?

These are some of the questions for which we will try and suggest an answer.

Early Written Sources

The Overthrow and Conquest of Britain by Gildas   [mid 6th c]

The Book of Aneurin (The Four Ancient Books of Wales)   [600]

The Ecclesiastical History of the English People
                   by the Venerable Bede   [731]

Historia Britonnum by Nennius   [9th c]

Annales Cambriae   [10th c]

The Annals of the Four Masters (Annala na gCeithre Mháistrí)   [1632–36]

The Black Book of Carmarthen (Llyfr Du Caerfyrddin)   [c. 125])

The Book of Tallsin (Tugtha Tall Sin)   [10th c]

The Mabinogion (Pedair Cainc y Mabinogi)   [c 12th c]

The Welsh Triads (Trioedd Ynys Prydein)   [13th c]

The Annals of Tiger Nath   [11th c]

The Annals of Ulster   [15th c]

The Annals of Ireland   [17th c]

Historia Gentis Scotorum by Hector Boece   [1527]

Arthur of the Britons

Who Was He?

'Arthur' was not a common name in Britain although there was a Roman name 'Artorius'. In Latin '*Arto*' and in Old Welsh '*Arth*' means 'bear' and *Arth Rig* or *Arth Ru* would mean the Bear Chief. The bear represents strength, power and fearlessness. It was an integral totem in Celtic religion – an animal who hibernates and is dormant for a long period in winter and then re-awakens in the Spring, resembling the Arthur of legend who is sleeping in Avalon and one day will rise again to save the Britons. Was a bear the symbol on his battle standard? At the battle of Badon it was recorded that '*no one rode down as many as himself*' so he was clearly powerful and strong. We still say of someone, 'He was a bear of a man'. Was 'Arthur' a '*nom de guerre*', an epithet like 'the Lion', or 'Braveheart'? The 6th century writer Gildas talks of a man who was charioteer to 'The Bear'. Is this perhaps a reference to Arthur?

Cavalry Patrol
Johnny Shuman

Whatever his real name, Arthur seems to have been well connected. He was probably a grandson of Ceretic who ruled Alt Clut (Strathclyde) from around 420 to 475 and made it the most powerful and wealthiest of the northern tribes. Although Arthur is not mentioned in the King Lists, the evidence for this connection is that Arthur's heirs were great-grandsons of Ceretic and his sister was married to Lot of the Gododdin, the other most powerful tribe of the north who occupied the area from the Forth to the Tweed.

Growing Up

As a British warrior aristocrat, Arthur's life would have centred on hunting, fishing and soldiering. He would not have been raised by his blood parents but, as was the custom, would have been sent away for fostering by another family in another sept or clan. The foster father was responsible for providing an all round education. While academic learning and artistic achievement were important, the first priority was learning the martial arts. Fostering, like marriage, created the network of inter-familial relationships which bonded society.

Breaking those bonds through betrayal or adultery was the ultimate crime. Because it destroyed social cohesion and created anarchy, it was therefore treated as treason and punishable by death.

The Britons listed 'Four and Twenty Games' which the young warrior was expected to master.

'Six Feats of Activity' included throwing weights, running, leaping, swimming, wrestling and riding.

The 'Four Exercises of Weaponry' were archery and javelin throwing, swordsmanship, spear and buckler and quaterstaff. They would also learn dagger fighting and how to handle the single and two-handed axe. They were expected to master feats of dexterity such as sword juggling or spear vaulting (thrusting the butt in the ground and vaulting over the top), agility (the standing high jump), strength (tossing the caber) and lastly voice (the battle cry).

There were 'Three Rural Sports' – hunting, fishing and hawking, and their dogs (ancestors of today's deerhounds and wolfhounds) were also trained as dogs of war to go into battle with the cavalry.

'Seven Domestic Games' included musicianship, poetry, heraldry and diplomacy, and 'Four Board Games' 'like draughts, chess and *brandab* were strategy games to sharpen the mind. Games were also important for developing the skills needed for survival in combat. For example, shinty provided ideal practice for the fast moving mêlées of the battlefield.

Four horsemen
Meigle Museum

Arthur's apprenticeship would have started around the age of eight to ten years old and, on graduating to adulthood, he would have had to prove himself as a young warrior by participating in a raid and returning with a trophy.

He would then have joined a chief's war band or more probably the Manau cavalry. In return for his military skill, he would have been rewarded with good equipment, mead, feasts and eloquent tributes for his valour by the bards. The warriors were an elite band of brothers – living, eating, sleeping, fighting and dying together. They were the heroes of their age, bound by a strict code of honour.

Fighting was essentially seasonal – campaigning in the summer months between sowing and reaping and using the winter as a time for training and preparation. A Roman writer of the 1st century AD wrote 'the whole nation…is war mad, both high spirited and ready for battle, but otherwise simple and not uncultured'. Fighting was a way of life and the adolescent excesses of young men away from home were regarded more as having a bit of fun and winning their spurs. If caught raiding cattle, it might end up as a challenge in single combat. Occasionally people were killed but not in any great number.

Social Organisation

The Celtic way of life was common to all the Celtic tribes – Britons, Scots and Picts. The Britons north of Hadrian's Wall had never been Romanised. Even south of the Wall, the centralised, urban-based Roman system had only been an organisational veneer. Celtic tribal society was its complete opposite – a network of rural, semi-autonomous cells, knitted together by a system of communal bonding.

Kinship was the key. Four generations, all descended from a great grandfather, constituted a family group. Everyone in that group shared in inheritance and was jointly responsible for the behaviour of everyone else. If one of them committed a misdemeanour, the case would come before a travelling Druid jurist. If found guilty, the whole group would be obliged to contribute to the fine but this would be divided up into different amounts, assessed on a sliding scale, according to the proximity of the relationships. Payment would be in cattle (Roman coinage rapidly went out of use for domestic exchange although it continued to be used in international trade). The ultimate punishment was banishment from the tribe.

A cow with a bell
Pictavia

The tribes were ruled by a Paramount or High Chief. The Anglo-Saxons termed them 'Kings', but they were not kings in the feudal sense of governing a territory. A Chief was head of a people, not the ruler of a place. This concept carried through eventually into the Kingdom of Scotland, whose monarchs were Kings of Scots, never Kings of Scotland. Nor was the High Chief a lawgiver. New laws were proposed and adopted by the people in assembly. The legal system was independent of the Chief and administered by the Druids. It was so comprehensive that it was later adopted by both Angle and Viking settlers as being better than their own. A primary royal court would be maintained as a capital but it was not

Top:
A hunter with shield and spear at Eassie Churchyard, Angus

Bottom:
A hunter on horseback with a hound chasing wild boar
Pictavia

an administrative centre like a Roman city. There were multiple courts throughout his territory and, like the Druids, the high chief would travel round.

Each High Chief would have his own full time military force with warriors drawn from these upper echelons of the clan hierarchy. They provided stability and guaranteed the safety of the commoners to till the soil and make the goods

Succession to the high chiefdom was not inherited by primogeniture of birth (hereditary kingship was an idea introduced to Britain by the Romans). Instead, the clan chiefs of the tribe represented a pool of aristocrats of equal status and they would elect whom they considered the most able. Each clan was made up of septs or sub clans, each headed by a chieftain. Their importance was essentially social and legal.

The middle class were liable to be called upon for military service but they were territorials and only made up the numbers of foot soldiers when needed. They also provided the full-time batmen to wait on the warrior nobility.

Then came the commoners who were legally forbidden to fight.

At the lowest level of society were the slaves who had been won in war and provided field labour.

Class divisions were not rigid and it was possible for families to move up or down the social ladder. It was a rural society. The bulk of the population scraped by on subsistence agriculture with a mixture of arable cultivation and stock rearing. The country north of Hadrian's Wall was heavily forested so the people lived in clearings. Their small farming settlements were clusters of round huts with thatched roofs, enclosed within a wooden palisade. The farm would also include a husking and winnowing floor, a granary and drying racks. The main hut might have had a souterrain (an underground chamber that could be used for storage or in times of danger serve as a place of refuge).

Reconstruction of a Celtic Homestead at Rochester, Northumberland

Through tribute, they supported the warrior aristocracy who led a life of relative luxury and leisure. In the Chief's hall, they passed their days feasting, training and hunting together. Hunting was an important social pastime – sometime with spears on horseback using horns and packs of hounds, and sometimes stalking wild boar with crossbows.

Religion

People lived in harmony with the natural environment that surrounded them. Everything in nature was a revelation of God. They had no fear either of the power of the elements, nor awe of the beauty of the Earth because they were not questionable. It was all part of Creation.

Before the coming of Christianity, kinship was not only the basis of social interaction between the living, but also with the dead. Ancestor worship is not a religion you can join. There can be no question of conversion to a faith and you are either born into a genealogy or you are not. The spirit is eternal, the soul does not die, it just passes on into other bodies. Life and death are a single continuum. The mortal world is paralleled by an immortal world – so there is no fear of death because you simply cross over. This is why the deceased were buried with useful items to take with them on their passage from one world to the other

The ancestors can assist the living, although they cannot always respond immediately as they are often busy with their own existence. There are, however, times in the year when the two worlds come closer together and contact is easier. Relics would be carefully kept – skulls were particularly important. These would be brought out at times of interaction when food would be shared with the dead and favoured dishes of the recently deceased would feature at the feast.

Alongside the ancestors were the heavenly powers of the sun, moon and stars which regulated the earth and enabled druids to calculate with great exactitude, the seasons and the years.

Matching these were Mother Earth and the Green Man, representing the regeneration of life and abundance. These were found in the sacred groves of the forest, in solitary places where man is alone with the elements, in the animal world of the horned god and in the depths of the waters. In the legend where Arthur has Excalibur thrown into the waters of the lake, he is, as present day archaeology has revealed, simply following an ancient Celtic custom of appeasing the Gods.

Arthur was Christian. Priests and missionaries gradually replaced the religious role of the Druids but the importance of ancestry and kinship remained the basis of social organisation and the old festivals were simply adapted and integrated into the new religion.

An abandoned Celtic homestead at Rochester, Northumberland

The Roman Legacy

Arthur was a Celt living in a part of Britain that had never been Romanised; yet his military background was essentially shaped by the Roman military tradition. In the years immediately preceding their final departure, the cavalry he commanded had originally been formed, trained and equipped by the Romans to patrol and defend the Pictish frontier. To understand Arthur's Britain, we need to understand the conditions which created it.

When the Romans invaded Britain, there was no Scotland, England or Wales. Britain was a conglomeration of Celtic tribes who spoke a common Brythonic language, albeit with regional dialects. The Pictish tribes who lived north of the Forth/Clyde valley are believed to have spoken an earlier form of the language. The Picts were settled mainly in the fertile straths in the east of the country. During their three and a half centuries of occupation, the Romans had tried to conquer the whole of Britain but they had never succeeded in subduing the Picts.

The Picts were masters of guerrilla hit and run tactics and had proved a constant thorn in the Roman flesh throughout the whole period of their occupation, not only raiding by land, but also by sea, and capable, with their huge fleet, of mounting lightning attacks to persistently pillage the Roman coastline.

Hadrian's Wall
Reconstruction at
Vindolanda

The Emperor Hadrian had built the Wall which straddled Britain from Newcastle to Carlisle. Twice the Romans had tried to advance to a line from the Forth to the Clyde where they built a second wall, the Antonine Wall, and twice, after a few years, they had been forced to abandon it.

During the 4th century, the Pictish raids were augmented by the arrival of Anglo-Saxon pirates. The Romans built a chain of coastal watchtowers. With their regular army in Britain seriously undermanned, they began to rely on mercenaries recruited from the Angle and Saxon territories in Germany.

It all came to a head in 367 when an alliance of Picts, Scots, Irish Attacoti*, Saxons and Franks attacked simultaneously from North, South, East and West. In return for a share of the loot, the Roman auxiliaries operating as scouts north of the Wall had not only failed to provide any warning but had also given the enemy vital military information on the strengths and positions of the depleted Roman forces.

The severely undermanned Roman garrisons were overwhelmed and, for a year, the invaders sacked and pillaged the whole of Britain. It was known as the Great Conspiracy. Eventually, Roman reinforcements arrived from the continent. Order was restored under General Theodosius and in 369 Britain was reorganised.

Model of Roman Fort at Vindolanda

---

* Suggestions are that the Attacotti may have been people from Alt Clut (Strathclyde) or from the Northern or Western isles, but no one knows.

- South of the wall there were four provinces:
  - South of a line from the Severn to the Thames was **Britannia Prima**.
  - North of this to a line from the Mersey to the Humber was known as **Flavia Caesariensis**.
  - From this line up to the Wall was **Maxima Caesariensis** – a military zone.
  - Wales was **Britannia Secunda**.
  - North of the Wall, beyond the limits of the Empire, covering the area between the Hadrian and Antonine Walls, was a fifth but autonomous province – **Valentia**

> Theodosius restored to its former state, a province which was recovered, that he had previously abandoned to enemy rule. This he did to the extent that it had a properly appointed governor, and it was from that time onwards known as 'Valentia' by decision of the Emperor.
>
> AMMIANUS XXVIII.III

The base of Hadrian's Wall at Steel Rig just above Vindolanda

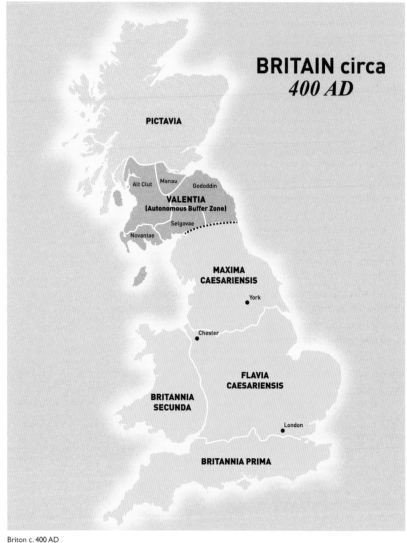

BRITAIN circa
400 AD

PICTAVIA

Alt Clut   Manau
                    Gododdin
VALENTIA
(Autonomous Buffer Zone)
        Selgovae
Novantae

MAXIMA
CAESARIENSIS

York

Chester

FLAVIA
CAESARIENSIS

BRITANNIA
SECUNDA

London

BRITANNIA PRIMA

Briton c. 400 AD
Arno Vilanove

The territory between the Antonine and Hadrian's Wall was inhabited by four tribes. In what is now the Scottish Southern Uplands lived the Selgovae (the hunters). We do not know their Celtic name for themselves. They occupied an area of dense and impenetrable Caledonian forest. In the south, the Cheviots joined up with the Pennines. In the west, in what is present day Dumfrieshire, they were bordered by the Galwyddel (in Latin *Novantae*), a tribe occupying Galloway and the Isle of Man.

The east coast from Newcastle-on-Tyne up to the Firth of Forth was the land of the **Gododdin** (or, in Latin, the *Votadini*). Their capital was on Traprain Law in West Lothian – a 40-acre site on top of a 500ft high hill which was enclosed by a massive earthen rampart.

Excavations at the Gododdin capital on Traprain Law (Dunpender) in East Lothian reveal the construction of an additional outer stone rampart. Also, at this time, a mass of silver treasure was buried beneath the floor of a house – an indication of serious instability. The treasure was discovered during an excavation in 1919. There were more than a hundred items bundled as if for melting down. It has been suggested that the silver may have been payment from the south but packaged as bullion due to lack of adequate coinage. It is now on display in the National Museum of Scotland.

Archaeology indicates that the Gododdin had a special status during the Roman period. Brooches, pottery, glass and metalwork, including such exotic items as tweezers, nail cleaners and ear scoops, were the debris of a sophisticated aristocracy who for a long time enjoyed access to imported goods of the highest quality.

Photograph by Alexander Curle of the Horde at the time of the discovery in 1920

Most of the Pictish border, from the top of Loch Lomond in the west across the foothills of the highland glens to Doune just east of Stirling, was controlled by **Alt Clut** (in Latin *Damnoni* – the miners) who governed what is now Dumbartonshire, Ayrshire, Renfrewshire and Lanarkshire ('Clut' has become 'Clyde').

Antonine Wall at
Watling Lodge

The enemy to the north were two groups of Pictish tribes – one south of the Grampians, the other to the north.

Money now poured into the new autonomous province of Valentia enabling them to strengthen their defenses. Possibly at this time, the Catrail (or Picts Work Dyke) was repaired and reinforced. This was a ditch and bank probably with wooden palisades which started on what is now the English border in the heart of the Cheviots and ran for 50 miles north to the Tweed – along what may have been the Selgovae border.

The Gododdin on the east coast seems to have been split into two prefectures, one north and the other south of the Tweed. They not only had the job of protecting the northern frontier and the east coast but also of patrolling their western boundaries and keeping the unruly Selgovae bottled up within the Central Uplands.

There was also a narrow coastal strip running to the Upper Forth to include the area round Stirling and Clackmannan on the northern shore. This area was called **Manau**. It covered an area just behind and just in front of the Antonine Wall.

The Romans recorded that Theodosius retook 'the place which owed allegiance to Rome and from that time forward this was called Valentia in honour of the emperor and his brother'. The phrase '*owed allegiance to Rome*' implies a

Protectorate. The Gododdin, the Alt Clut and Galwyddel each became *feodorati* – self-governing tribes with their own administration and laws but now under a Roman Prefect (*praefectus gentium*) who ran the system with a local council of *decurions* (local landowners or sub-chiefs who administered public works and collected local taxes.)*
Theodosius not only strengthened Hadrian's Wall but also restored the Antonine Wall and the ports which supplied it at Dumbarton in the West and Camlann in the East. Manau seems to have been a military zone directly under the command of military HQ in York.

To co-ordinate defence, and maintain law and order, Theodosius created small rapid reaction detachments of cavalry garrisoned in the three tribal territories and in Manau. These were full-time professionals who fought and thought like a Roman force but spoke Old Welsh (Brythonic) rather than Latin and whose commanders, although appointed by the Roman military governor in York, were drawn from the native British aristocracy. The King Lists suggest that after the Roman withdrawal their descendants became the ruling dynasties of their tribes. In Manau the commander was Padarn Beisrudd ap Tegid – Padarn of the Scarlet Cloak, son of Tegid. This suggests that he was Roman British and of high rank – perhaps the most senior of the commanders – with a crack unit which, more than a century later, would be inherited by Arthur. Little is known about the Manau. It only appears in passing references but it seems to have maintained its own autonomy and by the sixth century may have had a closer relationship with Alt Clut rather than Gododdin.

Stirling was the headquarters and a bridgehead. To the west, the boglands of Flanders Moss were difficult but not impassable. They stretched all the way to the Lake of Menteith. Eastwards, the river Forth was navigable and presented a major barrier. So the River crossing at Stirling was the gateway between north and south and, as such, was highly strategic.

---

* Four years later, Theodosius employed the same strategy with troublesome tribes on the African borders of the Empire.

Based on the Roman system, the cavalry would have had strength of around 480 men per cohort, each led by a Squadron Leader. These were subdivided into troops of 32 men, with a lieutenant, sergeant and corporal. They were armed with a long cutting sword (a Roman *spatha*) used for slashing and an oval shield. They also carried a spear with a wooden shaft and a diamond shaped head, and probably an axe, a dagger and a sling.

Everyday wear consisted of a knee-length tunic, long trousers tied at the waist and the ankles and a warm cloak of wool or skins held by a clasp brooch. Over the tunic, the cavalry wore another knee-length tunic made of leather with a coat of chain mail belted at the waist. The helmet was basically a leather cap covered in metal with neck and ear guards riveted on and with flexible cheek pieces. The standard bearers wore an animal skin with a head. It is possible that Arthur's standard bearer may have had a bear (*art* in Welsh,) and that this gave him his *nom de guerre*.

The horses were small and sturdy, around 12 to 15 hands. Their descendants still roam the Cumbrian Fells.

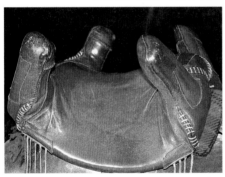

Roman cavalry saddle

Unarmoured but decorated with pendants and discs, there were no stirrups but a four-horned saddle locked the rider in place. Pictish sculptures reveal that the horses 'paced' – a running movement where the legs on the nearside move together in one direction while the legs on the offside move in the other. This smoothes out the ride. Unlike the trot, there is no need for the rider to post up and down and so it is less tiring to both horse and rider, allowing greater distances to be covered quickly.

When the Roman legions finally left for good in 410, the northern cavalry represented the only professional mounted force in the whole of Britain. South of Hadrian's Wall, the native Britons had not been allowed to bear arms for over 300 years.

Post Roman Britain 410–490

The area north of Hadrian's Wall and south of the Pictish frontier was a land covered in dense forest, with marshy boglands in the river valleys. The entire population would have been less than half of present day Edinburgh. The effect of the Roman withdrawal was minimal. Organised in four tribes, they had remained autonomous and although they had benefitted from trade and learned Roman military skills, their way of life had hardly been affected. They mostly lived in dispersed farming settlements of extended families.

Each tribe had its capital and a network of defensive forts. There were no towns but there were ports which still traded internationally.

People travelled abroad and the network of Roman roads which was still in place made travel, throughout Britain and beyond, both fast and easy.

South of Hadrian's Wall, down to a line from the Humber to the Mersey, had been a zone of military occupation where Romanisation had been superficial but where, in spite of the withdrawal of the legions, a degree of army infrastructure and training had survived.

In Southern Britain, below the Humber/Mersey line, it was a very different story.

Here, the Romans had imposed a hierarchical administration on the traditional tribal society of the native Britons. Authority had been centralised in a network of new towns. These were the centres of administration, trade and law, and from which all roads, both geographical and administrative, led to Rome. Bureaucracy, urbanisation and centralised government were the key to the Roman system. Defence had been entirely the responsibility of the imperial forces so there was no indigenous military tradition. This is where resistance to invasion was at its weakest.

After 410, the Roman system rapidly became dysfunctional. Local squabbles and the arrival of the plague in the 440s further added to the collapse. The Roman system did not disappear overnight but it was gradually replaced as the traditional Celtic system of decentralised government re-emerged.

Southern Britain after 410

Whatever was left of central government in the South of Britain was held together under a traditional Celtic High Chief – Vortigern. He was supported by a council of representatives and a body of ex-Roman mercenary troops – mostly Anglo-Saxons, who continued as an operational force as long as they were paid. But by 436, the money had run out. The rich underbelly of Britain was ripe for the picking. In the southeast, the Pictish raids were becoming intolerable. Britain had depended entirely on the Roman navy and had no fighting ships of her own. In desperation, Vortigern looked to Europe. In 429 he invited Hengest and Horsa, two Saxon mercenaries, to help him defend his coastline. In return he agreed to feed and clothe them and gave them settlers rights on the Isle of Thanet in the Thames estuary.

Hengest quickly realised that Southern Britain was open for the taking and set about ingratiating himself with Vortigern. First he offered Vortigern his daughter in marriage. Vortigern took the bait and fell madly in love. Then Hengest suggested, 'If you like, I will send for my son and his brother, both valiant men who, if I ask them, will fight against the Picts and you can give them lands in the north, near the Antonine Wall.' The idea of giving the Picts a dose of their own medicine with a raid on their home naval bases in the north, appealed greatly. In due course, Hengest's two sons arrived with a fleet of 40 ships. 'In these they sailed round the country of the Picts, laid waste the Orkneys and took possession of many regions, even to the Pictish confines'.

Vortigern died, or more likely was assassinated, in the middle of the century and a new military commander, Ambrosius Aurelianus took over the leadership of British resistance. He was probably based in Wiltshire, and for the first time, defeated Hengest. But nevertheless the Saxons continued to expand their territory in Essex, Sussex and eventually Wessex from whence there were mass emigrations of Britons to Armorica (Brittany) and Galicia. It should be remembered that France and Spain were not foreign territories. Although Latin was the lingua franca of the old Empire, they were also Celts and spoke a similar dialect of the Old Welsh language of the Britons. For nearly 400 years they had been part of the same empire with Latin as a lingua franca – so emigration and assimilation were not so daunting.

By 461, the entire southeast of present-day England had been lost to the Saxons. In Europe, the Western Roman Empire was in total collapse. Goths, Visigoths, Franks, Vandals and Huns poured over the old frontiers, burning, raping and pillaging. And in 476, Rome itself was taken.

Northern Britain after 410

North of the Humber/Mersey line, the old military zone which stretched up to Hadrian's Wall was governed from York (Ebrauc) by the Dux Britannicum – a man called Coel Hen ('Old Coel' hence the nursery rhyme Old King Cole). He was a Briton, but Roman trained, and although the legions had left, he still had British and Angle detachments at his command. After the Roman withdrawal, he continued to exercise the same authority as before but now ruled as a tribal High chief. He reintroduced the Celtic tribal system of inheritance so that his territory would be subdivided between his sons and their descendants. It is from this time onwards that the genealogies also record a line of High Chiefs for the Gododdin and another line for the Alt Clut.

The Dux Brittanicum in York was also responsible for relations with the

The Mannan Stone now in Clackmannan, but originally a standing stone which stood near the shore on the Manau/Pictish boundary and is believed to havebeen dedicated to a sea god

semi-autonomous Chiefdoms north of Hadrian's Wall. For as long as they were paid, the cavalry force in the Manau around the head of the Upper Forth estuary would have continued to report directly to Coel Hen in York.

The original commander of the Manau cavalry Paternus Pesrut ('the man in the red cloak') was succeeded first by his son and then by his grandson, Cunedda.

Cunedda was connected through one of his grandmothers to a chiefdom in North Wales which was now in trouble. In the 380s, the Roman garrisons in North Wales had been withdrawn, leaving it open to invasion from Ireland. The Scots, who at this time were a tribe based in Northern Ireland, had gradually established settlements along the west coast of Wales from Anglesey to Pembroke.

Cunedda was married to a daughter of Coel Hen. In around the 420s, Coel Hen may have sent word or the offer may have come directly from Wales, that if the Manau cavalry could expel the Scots, they would be rewarded with the retaken Welsh lands and titles.

The network of Roman roads was still intact so travel from Manau to North Wales was fast and easy. Accompanied by eight of his nine sons, Cunedda is said to have led a force of 900 cavalry to the aid of the Welsh. They expelled the Scots 'with enormous slaughter so that they never came back to live there again'.

Dere Street still runs from Edinburgh

Cunedda and his sons founded a dynasty which endured eight centuries and only ended with the defeat of Llewellyn the Great by Edward 1 of England in 1282/83. Cunedda means 'Great Leader'. He gave his name to Gwynedd, his son Caraticus to Cardigan and another son, Meirion, to Meirrionydd.

There is a school of thought which, if one takes the dates in Nennius' *Hostorium Brittonim* as factual, places the invasion much earlier in the final decades of the 5th century and attributes it to Paternus of the Red Cloak. In this scenario, Cunedda is credited with reorganising Gwynedd into sub-chiefdoms and laying the foundations for its future power.

Cunedda's eldest son Typaun is recorded as inheriting the command in the Manau.

When Typaun died, there is no information as to who succeeded him or how and why, towards the end of the century, Arthur was chosen to take over but it is recorded that on his mother's side, he was a great great grandson of Cunedda. Arthur clearly no longer reported to the Roman HQ in York. But this crack cavalry unit continued its role as a rapid reaction force – full time professionals with the power to police civil unrest and quell any threat of invasion from the North.

Cunedda's Invasion of Wales
Wikipedia

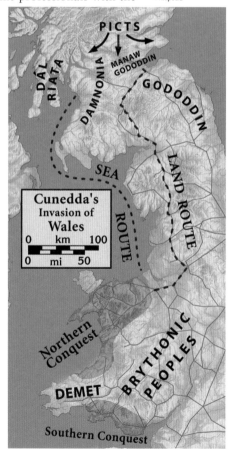

From a military point of view, Arthur inherited the Roman tradition in training, tactics and equipment. But as a Briton, his world and his culture was Celtic. Although we talk of Picts, Scots, Angles, Saxons and the various chiefdoms of 'The Men of the North', we should remember that these were not 'nation states'. It is the Anglo Saxon Chronicle which calls them 'kingdoms'. Clans or tribes are a better description. They were all loose confederations of kinship groups.

The tribes were a network of different family groups which acted independently. So an invasion by Picts, Scots or Angles does not imply a nationally coordinated attack by a foreign power – but rather a raid by a particular group, or alliance of groups, acting on their joint initiative for their common benefit. And when they were not warring across tribal borders, they were squabbling amongst themselves. It was a way of life which had existed for centuries. It was quite possible for trade to be taking place between different tribes while other groups of the same tribes were at war. Trading and raiding ran side by side.

In addition, there were cross-border marriages and there were families of European and even Near Eastern origin, descended from soldiers of the Roman army or merchants who had retired and settled on both sides of the Wall. Armies were small. Cunedda's 900 horse had been enough to expel the entire Scots population from the coastal areas of Wales. The 'Invincible Army' of the sons of Old King Coel are recorded as being 300 spearmen. At the decisive battle of Catterick when the Gododdin finally fell to the Angles, their mounted force was only 300 handpicked men.

The battle formation would depend on the enemy deployment and the lie of the land, but the senior champions would be in the front rank with less experienced warriors behind. Battle horns sounded commands over the din of the fighting, and on the sidelines, the bards observed the events as they unfolded, recording special deeds of individual heroism or of cowardice.

Christianity

Arthur was a Christian and a crusader. He went into battle with God on his side and a cross on his shield. The Church had been another, subtle Roman innovation. The new religion introduced a moral justification for political authority by divine right. As the military strength of the Empire declined, God stepped into the breach.

From the Venerable Bede we learn that more than a century earlier, in 387, St Ninian had brought Christianity to the Galwyddel. Ninian, who was probably born in Galwyddel, had spent a decade or so in Rome where he had been ordained first as a priest and then as a bishop. Returning across Europe to start his mission in Galloway, he had stopped at Tours where the bishop, estimating some of the difficulties that would face him, gave him twelve monks – skilled carpenters and masons, already well-schooled in monastic life. The Bishop was called Martin. Some time later, as a small stone church gradually took shape on an island off the Galloway coast, the news came of Bishop Martin's death. To honour him Ninian dedicated his new foundation to Saint Martin. Locally however it had become known as *Hwith-aern* (the White House) because of the whitish stone with which it was built – hence the modern name 'Whithorn'.

But how true is this account? The Venerable Bede's *Ecclesiastical History of the English People* was completed four years before his death in 735. It was written in Northumberland where Bede had no access to local tradition in Galloway and was dependent for his information on a revision of an earlier Whithorn document. In the process of transcription, there may have been a scribal error when a 'U' was rewritten as an 'N' – not so easy to imagine in print but very easy when handwritten. Was 'Nin(n)ian' actually 'Uin(n)iau' in Old Welsh (also known as Guinnion) and 'Finnian' in Gaelic? Uinniau was a Briton and a Bishop and there is a record of an encounter with a High Chief Tudwal or Tutguall, of the Alt Clut who appears to have been responsible for the annexation of the Galwyddel. What is certain is that there was a monastery at Whithorn which was a major centre for training missionaries who went out to spread the word on both sides of the Irish Sea, and it was in one of their centres in Ireland that St Columba was trained.

Whithorn was taken over by the Northumbrian Church in the early 8th century when the Gododdin fell to the Angles of Northumbria. At this point the life of Uinniau (Ninian) was undoubtedly doctored to accord with the pretentions of the Northumbrian Church and its propaganda that because Uinniau (Ninian) had been responsible for first converting the Southern Picts, that they should come under Northumbrian (Angle) jurisdiction

The cult of St Ninian did not really start until the 12th century. If Uinniau worked with the Southern Picts,

as believed, he would undoubtedly have spent time in Manau. It is no coincidence that there is a parish south of Stirling which bears the name of St Ninian and traces its origins back to the 5th century, although until the 12th century it was simply known as Eccles (from the Latin *ecclesia*).

By Arthur's time, at the turn of the 6th century, there was almost certainly a strong Christian presence

Top Left and Right:
St Ninian's Cave
Isle of Whithorn

Above:
Foundations of St
Ninian's church
Whithorn

Right:
Candida Casa
Isle of Whithorn

throughout the tribal areas of the The Men of the North (Yr Hen Ogled). The notable exception were the Selgovae who remained firmly traditional. Christianity was also well established amongst the Southern Picts where Saint Palladius was a missionary in the second half of the 5th century. Saint Serf, who is said to have been ordained by Uinnaiu (Ninian), founded an abbey at Culross on the northern shore of the Forth and there was a regular missionary traffic across the Pictish frontier.

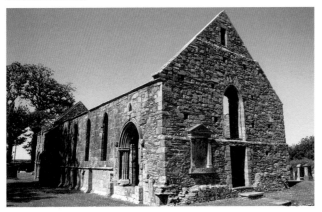

Ruins of the medieval Whithorn Priory

Alt Clut

The Alt Clut (Strathclyde) capital was at Dumbarton (*Dun Breatan*) on top of an unscalable twin-peaked rock. The river Clyde and the steepness of the rockface made elaborate defences unnecessary except on the landward side, where a spur of land provided a bridge to the mainland at low tide and where a timber fronted rampart of rubble and earth ran along the base of the rock. The rampart was two and a half metres thick and two metres high, topped by a wooden and wicker palisade. The fortress, was a strong military defence, and also looked imposing. It was a symbol of strength and status. And where there was a centre of secular power, there was also a seat of religious power.

In the last days of the Romans, the High Chief of **the Alt Clut** (Strathclyde) was Ceretic (in Latin *Coroticus*). He converted to Christianity and his family's collaboration with

Dun Breatan today (top)
and as it might have
appeared c.500 (bottom)
– capital of Alt Clut'.
Tandem

the Romans brought great wealth – indeed he was known as Ceretic *Hael*, meaning Ceretic the 'rich'. When the 'overseas aid' from Rome dried up, he diversified into the slave trade, raiding Ireland and selling captured Scots to the Picts.

Word reached St Patrick in Ireland. St Patrick had been born in the in 387 at a place called *Banna Venta Berniae*. This could either be present day Kilpatrick or the Roman forts of Birdoswald (in Latin *Banna*) at the west end of the Wall or Ravenglass (in Latin *Glannoventa)* on the Cumbrian coast. Whichever the case, he was a Man of the North.

In his mid-teens he had been captured by Scots raiders and taken back to their homeland in Antrim as a slave. So slavery was a matter close to his heart and he sent a letter of excommunication to Ceretic.

When Ceretic died in the latter half of the century he was succeeded by his grandson.

Dumbarton Rock from the west

The Selgovae and Galwyddel

To the south of the Alt Clut, present day Dumfries and Galloway were still the land of the Selgovae and the Novantae (or Galwyddel.) **The Selgovae** kept themselves to themselves in the densely forested Southern Uplands.

With the disappearance of Roman sea trade, **the Galwyddel** were isolated and weakened. Both tribes would shortly disappear, swallowed up by their more powerful northern neighbours. The Galwyddel appear to have been annexed around 485 – although their old ruling family survived independently on the Isle of Man until the time of the Vikings.

We know all this because apart from the early written histories, there are also written genealogies, – the lists of the rulers of various chiefdoms, traditionally recited and remembered by the bards of the 'Y Goggled' – 'Men of the North'. These however, are names without dates so there is a degree of inexactitude as to when they reigned.

The Gododdin

In the east, the equally wealthy **Gododdin** were reinforced on their northern flank by the cavalry of Manau. The Gododdin territory, which traditionally straddled the Wall stretching from the Tees to the Forth, had been administered as two Roman prefectures. These now became two British High Chiefdoms.

The area from the Tweed to the Forth was given to Lot who seems to have become the first independent Gododdin High Chief. He moved his capital from the centuries old Dunpender (Traprain Law) to Dun Eidyn (Edinburgh) and subsequently gave his name to present day Lothian. Dunpender remained important as a religious site. The Maidens Stone is a narrow vertical cleft between a rock that has split away from an adjacent outcrop. Passing through the cleft is still said to ensure a woman's fertility – a folk memory from pre-Christian times.

Top:
Dunpender (Traprain)
Law – a circular
structure

Middle:
Dunpender (Traprain
Law), the Gododdin
Capital from the west

Left:
Dunpender (Traprain)
Law – the water
reservoir

Top:
Base of stone rampart

Above:
Dun Eidyn (Edinburgh Castle)

The Bryneich

The old Gododdin territory south of the Tweed to the Tees formed the new chiefdom of **Bryneich.** (Northumberland). The first high chief was Coel's youngest son. This made good strategic sense. Lines of communication from the old capital at Dunpender (Traprain Law), just south of the Forth, were too extended and it was more effective to have a new command HQ at Dun Guayardi, the Gododdin name for present day Bamburgh.

Dun Guyardi
(Bamburgh Castle)

The Scots

At the beginning of the 5th century, the Scots were being squeezed out of their homeland in Antrim in Northern Ireland, so they had established a small colony in sparsely populated Pictish territory on the coast of present day Argyll. They called it **Dalriada**. They also tried to settle the Ayrshire coast. Coel sent raiding parties to steal their cattle, engineering it to look as if it was a raid by the Picts. The subterfuge backfired and the Scots and the Picts united to mount a joint attack on Alt Clut. Dumbarton called for help and Coel marched north.

The invaders retreated back into the hills and Coel set up camp beside the Ayrshire river since named after him – the Coyle.

Up in the hills, the Scots and Picts suffered and starved and for a long time were kept at bay. But then, unexpectedly, they launched a sudden last-ditch night attack. Coel and his army were caught off guard. They were overrun and routed. Trying to escape, Coel floundered into a bog and was drowned.

He was succeeded by his two sons who split his chiefdom south of the Wall into two. The Chiefdom of **Rheged** took in the area west of the Pennines and ran from the Mersey to the Solway. The other brother inherited the Chiefdom of **Ebrauc** based on York on the east side of the Pennines running from the Humber up to the Tyne.

By the time Arthur appeared on the scene at the end of the 5th century, the Scots had ruled settlements on the sparsely populated west coast of present day Argyll for over 150 years. But towards the end of the 5th century, their homeland in Antrim in Northern Ireland was under increasingly severe pressure and in about 460, Fergus had arrived with two brothers to expand their colonies in Scotland. The centre of power shifted from Antrim to this new land of Dalriada which now became the Scots homeland, with its new capital at Dunadd (four miles north east of Lochgilphead). They created three and later four sub-chiefdoms and brought with them the Stone of Destiny

Dunadd – capital of the Scots and scene of early coronations with the Stone of Destiny

and it was here that the future High Chiefs of Scots were crowned. In the rocky floor of the fort are the carved imprints of two feet. They clearly had a ritualistic significance. In the rites of accession to the chiefship, did they represent the new chief stepping into the old one's shoes?

Ritual footsteps and font in the rocks near the Dunadd summit

As High Chief, Fergus ruled the central chiefdom based on Arran, Jura, Kintyre, Bute and the Cowal peninsula. This brought him to the frontier of Alt Clut. In around 500 AD, a fresh wave of immigrants came across the Irish Sea. At some stage there seems to have been a peace treaty with Alt Clut who agreed their settlement of these sparsely populated lands in return for the supply of recruits to reinforce the Alt Clut army.

View to the bay where the ships arrived from Ireland

The entrance from below
and within the fort

Dunadd Above: The stone
base of the ramparts

The well

Cavalry attacking
spearmen
Pictavia

The Picts

The Picts, at this time, were united in two loose confederations, each with their own High Chief. Three tribes in the north made up Northern Picts and were essentially pagan. They were geographically separated by the Grampians from the four tribes of the Southern Picts, who were the senior branch and were at least partly Christian.

The Pictish frontiers with Alt Clut and Gododdin moved backwards and forwards slightly over the centuries but basically the Picts were raiders rather than colonists. The Pictish border seems to have run from just north of Loch Lomond, eastwards along Glengyle Water and Loch Katrine to the north of Doune where it marched with Manau. The main centres of power and population of the four tribes of the Southern Picts were the rich farmlands of Atholl and Perth and also in Angus and in Fife. Further west in the mountains, the land became more marginal and the population more sparse.

Manau controlled the main trade route to the north along the old Roman road to Crieff and possibly patrolled as far north as Dunblane and Braco, before skirting the Ochil Hills. On the Abbey Mount at Stirling there is a fort which quite possibly served as a forward base and look out, while Arthur's GHQ was probably on the Castle Rock.

The Picts derive their name from the early days of the Romans – the Latin *Picti* meaning the 'painted people'. This is thought to refer to their practice of tattooing their bodies. It is believed that the tattoos told the story of a person's lineage and gave them an instantly recognisable identity – particularly useful in battle.

Jutes And Saxons

In the far south, the Saxons and their Jute allies now controlled the British coast from Essex to Dorset.

The Angles

The Angles were firmly established in Norfolk and around the Wash. They had originally been brought in by the Romans as mercenaries, to man the lookout stations along the east coast. In return had been given the right to settle in an area at the head of the Humber estuary, called Deria. From the end of the 5th century Angle immigration swelled rapidly with new immigrants from overseas taking over East Anglia, from whence they constantly sought to colonise and gain a foothold around natural harbours on river estuaries further north.

There also appears to have been a small colony on the island of Lindisfarne, dating from Roman times, where Angle mercenaries, manning the east end of the Wall had been allowed to marry locally and settle when they retired. The community seems to have been well integrated and not considered a threat. The population grew only very slightly and were firmly in the shadow of the Chiefs of Bryneich in their fortress across the water at Dun Guayardi (Bamburgh). However they clearly had trading relations across the North Sea and south of the Humber; and raiding parties coming in from the sea would have probed the strength of Briton defences from time to time.

Lindisfarne

The name Lindisfarne implies that it was settled by people who migrated from Lindsey (Lincolnshire). Lindsey had also been settled by retired German mercenaries during Roman times. Around 480 it became a springboard for Anglian conquest south and westward to form what became the Angle kingdom of Mercia. In the north, the Humber presented a serious obstacle. The river ran inland to form a great swamp as far as the dense forests of the Pennines. So expansion in the north, with Holy Island as a beachhead, only seems to have been a major threat later, culminating in the Angle capture of Dun Guayardi in 547 AD. This was the founding of the kingdom of Northumberland and the beginning of the real threat to the Men of the North.

This was the state of Britain when Arthur appeared on the scene and took command in Manau.

Arthur's early relations with Lot, High Chief of the Gododdin, appear to have been strained. Theoretically, the Gododdin were overlords of Manau. In the early days, although Manau was a military zone, the Gododdin would have been responsible for the civil administration within it and for providing supplies of food and drink for the military force. It is likely that after the departure of the Romans, Manau took control of its own administration like any other chiefdom and perhaps Lot was not as generously supportive as Arthur would have hoped? The relationship was also potentially confrontational in that Arthur was Christian and Lot, at least in the early part of his reign, was pagan.

But Arthur's sister (or half-sister?) was Lot's queen and gradually she may have helped pour oil on troubled waters, because as time went by, relations improved. Lot's children were all brought up Christian and one of his sons, Mordred, was apprenticed to Arthur to learn the skills of warriorhood, (and ultimately would be responsible for Arthur's death).

With his sister providing a strong link by marriage to the Gododdin, it would therefore have made sense for Arthur to balance this relationship through marriage with his other neighbouring ruling family in the Alt Clut. Before Guinevere, he is said to have had a first wife who gave him three sons, but we know nothing about her or the sons.

By now Alt Clut was almost certainly more important and richer than the Gododdin. Certainly, in the early part of his career, Arthur seems to have been more active in the west rather than the east. For the middle half of the 5th century,

Alt Clut had been ruled by Ceretic who had extended his chiefdom right down to the Solway incorporating Galwyddel. But after his death he seems to have split his territory in a north/south divide between his two sons.

The result was a period of instability. Between 475 and 500, there were no less than five rulers, each reigning for about five years. Weakened by internal rivalries, Alt Clut perhaps provided Arthur with the best opportunity to win his spurs. In terms of what followed, Arthur clearly championed the southern claimants and perhaps this is an indication of his own origins. He was born more or less at the time of the annexation of the Galwyddel and if he had been brought up there, in the cradle of Christianity, it would explain not only his own intense faith but also that of his sister, married to Lot of the Gododdin. This would also make sense of the inheritance of the Manau by sons of the same branch of the family after his death.

The Arthurian Campaign 490–516

History and hypothesis

The Welsh historian Nennius tells us in his *Historia Brittonum*:

Then it was that the magnanimous Arthur, with all the chiefs and military force of Britain, fought against the Saxons. And although there were many more noble than himself, yet he was 12 times chosen their commander, and was as often conqueror... In all these engagements the Britons were successful...

The *Historia Brittonum* is no longer considered as the work of a single identifiable author. The Annales Cambriae (which contain Arthur's battles) and genealogies were added as an appendix in the 10th century. The whole thing is a complex work of compilations of historical annals and legends which had already been edited and altered by synchronising historians in the 7th and 8th centuries. The information therefore is unlikely to be unquestionably accurate.

Nennius is writing in the 8th century in Wales. When he writes of the 'Saxons' he is identifying the principle enemy of his times. The word 'Saxon' therefore should be interpreted in a generic sense like 'Sassenach' to cover the multiple invaders of earlier times (i.e. not just Saxons but Angles, Picts, and Scots as well).

Arthur's 12 battles were fought over a period at the very end of the 5th century and in the early years of the 6th. So where were they, who were they against and why were they fought? Compared with other periods, the Dark Ages in Britain have been largely neglected by archaeology and to date there is little archaeological evidence to help locate the battle sites. Nennius lists them by name but many of the Brythonic names he knew in the 6th century were replaced during Anglo Saxon and Viking occupation.

Horseman
Meigle Museum

Only etymological derivation can perhaps hint at where to start looking.

The question of who was fighting with or against whom is further complicated by the difficulties of accurate dating. This is made even more muddling because until the Synod of Whitby in the mid seventh century, the Celtic Church and the Roman Church calculated the calendar differently.

This part of the story is therefore the most conjectural and this is where the real detective work begins. Other writers have concentrated heavily on place names and there is a choice of possible locations in almost every corner of Britain where a name could apply. To make sense, one has

Scots Pines

also to look at how the places might fit into an evolving, overall military and political strategy. Campaigns were about defending and extending territory. With his fast moving, small but highly effective cavalry Arthur was capable, through carefully planned ambushes, of surprising and routing a force many times larger than his own. It was a strategy of 'surgical strikes'.

Previous writers have identified the principle enemy at the time, in the north, as the Angles but, as we have seen, they did not become a major threat north of the Wall until after the fall of Dun Guayardi in 547AD. The period we are looking at is 50 years earlier and the raison d'être of the Manau cavalry was and always had been to hold and defend the frontier of the British tribes – Yr Hen Ogledd – against the Picts. So while Angles may well come into the story, is it not unlikely that the principal threat at the beginning of his career was still the Picts. Were they the foe against whom he won his spurs and earned his reputation?

My suggestions for likely locations for the battles appear in normal type but I also append previous writers' alternative suggestions for each battle in smaller type.

The First Five Battles –
A Defensive Campaign?

'The first battle was at the mouth of a river which is called Glein'

NENNIUS 8TH C

This was fought around the end of the fifth century and there seem to be two good possibilities for the location:

a) **Glen Water in Ayrshire** flows unto the river Irvine. The stronghold of Dundonald, near the coast, contained a mixture of timber built roundhouses and straight-side buildings all enclosed in a timber laced stone rampart. It was almost certainly the seat of the sub-chief of Aeron (hence Ayr) which by now, like Galwyddel, had been absorbed into Alt Clut. The dividing line of the apparent rivalry between north and south for the High Chiefship would have found its midpoint on the river Irvine. Over 25 years of turbulence, there had been five successive High Chiefs with rivalry between two branches of the ruling family – one seemingly with a power base in the north, the other in the south. The Irvine was the midpoint. The last of the five High Chiefs, Caw, was from the north. One can speculate that his successor Dumnagual might have been based at Dundonald and, if not an elder brother, was closely related to Arthur. Did the battle of Glein lead to the deposition of Caw and the accession of Dumnagual as the new High Chief of Alt Clut?

From *Idyllis of the King* – Gustav Doré

If this were a family feud, why would Arthur get involved unless, of course, he had family connections? Was he related to the ruling family of the southern part of Alt Clut?

On the other hand, it has also been suggested that the battle could have been against a seaborne landing. The old Roman road from the coast to Avondale, Clydesdale and beyond, crossed a ford at the mouth of the Glen. It was an important trade route from the coast. The hillfort of Louden Hill, overlooking Glen Water, is also the site of a Roman fort which could have been reoccupied after they left. The Scots had certainly been a threat in the past, raiding cattle and capturing slaves and booty, and there was a new wave of emigration from Antrim around this period but the thrust was concentrated further north to consolidate the new colonies in Dalriada. Furthermore the Gaelic Annals record the existence of a body organising regular pay and outfitting for Scots, hired as mercenaries for the powerful Alt Clut Army. Alt Clut had allowed the Scots to settle peaceably on their thinly inhabited isles and peninsulas in the west in return for their manpower. So relations seem to have been cordial.

There are no surviving accounts nor, to date, any archaeological finds to indicate Scots or Pictish raids at this time but the lack of evidence does not mean that it did not happen.

The case for Glen Water in Ayrshire is strengthened by the presence of St Monenna and her maidens at Dundonald. Saint Monenna, the daughter of a Scots chief in Northern Ireland, was born in 432, probably the same year that Saint Ninian is supposed to have died (a date which does not correspond with Uinniau who dies much later). In 450, she came to Whithorn with eight 'maidens' and a widow who had a son. They received instruction in monastic life before going out as missionaries. There are three separate accounts of her life and all three agree on where she went with her group of 'maidens'. But the Lives of the Saints cannot be

Possible site of the First Battle beside the Glen Water in Ayrshire

taken at face value as historical accounts of actual events. They have to be recognised as church propaganda and it could well be that St Monenna and her Maidens never came to Scotland at all and their story is mixed in with somebody else (such as St Brigid).

However, if they did, we are told that they started in Galloway, before moving up to Dundonald (*Dundevenel*) in Ayrshire. Did she meet Arthur here? Did he persuade her to follow him up to Dumbarton where she also founded a monastery? (Remember that Whithorn had a mission at Inchinnan near Dumbarton). Arthur seems to have pursued a strategy of encouraging missionaries to establish a presence in territories under his control. A group of nun missionaries would have represented a moral authority to reinforce the peace. It was a strategy which had served the Romans well when their military power was stretched and could have been equally effective in a *pax arthuriana*.

Above:
7th century monastic bell at Fortingall

Below:
Clach nam Breatan

Bottom:
Alt Fionn Ghleann (the line of trees mark the river)

b) There is an alternative location. To the north of Loch Lomond, just above the Falls of Falloch, there is a dramatic ten-foot high marker stone – the *Clach nam Breatan* (Stone of the Britons). From the Pictish side it looks like a giant outstretched hand saying 'stop'. This marked the point where the lands of the Britons of Alt Clut, the Scots of Dalriada and the Southern Picts all met. Nowadays, Glen Falloch carries the main road and the West Highland railway north to Crianlarich and Fort William. It has always been a strategic pass and in Arthur's day was equally a gateway between north and south.

On the east side of the Falloch River is the Alt Criche (the Border Water). On its western slope, below the Clach nam Breatan, is the **Alt Fionn Ghleann** (meaning White Veil

From *Idyllis of the King* –
Gustav Doré

Water). 'Veil' is *glo* in Gaelic and *llen* (in Welsh pronounced chlen) is white. This runs into the River Falloch, so could this be the mouth of '*the river which is called Glein*'?

The area at the mouth of the Ghleann is still heavily wooded and would be difficult territory for cavalry – if the armies were only about 300 men, an ambush is conceivable. However, the Clach nam Breatan is 2,000 feet higher up and not visible from the mouth of the Ghleann. This suggests that the trackway was not in the bottom of the glen but higher up the hill where the forest would have been thinner and, while still being directly above the river mouth, the land is flatter. Ancient Celtic trackways always tended to favour the hilltops and higher ground. We know that this corner was, at the time, a major trouble spot. If it was as

Falls of Falloch the Briton/Pictish border

The North end of Loch Lomond

open as the grassy plateau of today, it would have been an ideal site for a battle and indeed this is supported by a record of a battle here a couple of hundred years later.

Alternative Sites

For the battle on the Glein, previous writers have made other suggestions.

c) Alistair Moffat, in his book *Arthur and the Lost Kingdoms*, proposes that this was probably fought in around 485AD in **Northumberland** where the **river Glen** joins the Till which rises in the Cheviots and is a tributary of the Tweed. The site is close to the fort of Gefrin on a flat-topped hill (now called Yeavering Bell) – a key ancient stronghold of the Gododdin which by Arthur's time had passed into the high chiefdom of Bryneich.

River Glen
Northumberland

About 17 acres were enclosed by a wooden palisade. It is just 15 miles from the Bryneich capital at Dun Guyardi (Bamburgh) and the Angle colony on Lindisfarne. Was this an Angle raid? Moffat suggests that Arthur could have used the old fort as a base camp to wait in concealment until the invaders crossed the river below. This was a standard cavalry tactic. When the invasion force was halfway across and split between the two banks of the river, the cavalry would charge down forcing them into deeper water and wreaking havoc on their undefended flanks. Nearby is a standing stone known as The Battle Stone. So there quite probably was a battle here with the Angles but perhaps more likely later, when they were seriously trying to take territory after the fall of Dun Guyardi (Bamburgh) and the founding of the Angle Kingdom of Bernicia in 547AD. As already explained, the evidence seems that while there was Angle activity in East Anglia, their main thrust at the end of the fifth century was into Mercia. Alternatively, of course, the battle could have been to counter a seaborne Pictish raid. But in either case it is a long way inland.

Holy Island – site of the
Angle settlement

d) A further suggestion is the mouth of the **River Glen in Lincolnshire**. This marked the front line of Angle settlement around the Wash. In any battle here Arthur would have been allied with the Chiefdom of Ebrauc (York) centred on Coel's old capital at York. In which case, perhaps this was the beginnings of a combined force which later was to become known as 'The Great Invincible Army' (of which more later). But if Arthur's primary role was to defend the Pictish frontier, is it likely, at the very outset of his command, that he would be inclined to stray so far south of Hadrian's Wall?

Nennius continues:

'The second, third, fourth and fifth were beyond another river which is called Dubglass in the district of Linnius'

Dubglass can be interpreted as 'dark river' and *Linnius* as 'region of water'. The Lennox Forest, on the northern frontier of Alt Clut, also stretched to the Gareloch Peninsula on the west side of Loch Lomond. This, more than any other, is a 'region of water' and a few miles further north, about a mile downstream from the River Ghleann, there is the River Dubh Eas. The mouth of the Dubh Eas is flat land. Today it is open and farmed.

Also flowing into Loch Lomond on the narrow neck between Loch Lomond and Long Long is Glen Douglas with the river Douglas. Is this the river Nennius is

Left:
Glen Falloch

Right:
The river Dubh Eas

referring to? Both the Douglas and the Dubh Eas are within *the district of Linnius* (Lennox).

On the other hand, perhaps Dubglass is just a general reference for the southern boundary of the most northerly sept or subchiefdom of Alt Clut?

Why would there have been a battle here? After the departure of the Romans, Alt Clut had remained both stable and powerful under two successive High Chiefs. After the death of the second High Chief in 475, it seems to have been an ongoing power struggle with a succession of five High Chiefs over the next 26 years, alternating between the ruling families of the Northern and the Southern Alt Clut with each ruling for short five year periods. This internal rivalry dissipated resources and weakened the frontier.

At the turn of the century, the High Chief was called Caw. He appears to have ruled from 495 until he was deposed in 501 after having been defeated by the Picts. Was he deposed after the battle of Glein? Was this indeed in Ayrshire? Was it the culmination of the Alt Clut power struggle between north and south and was Arthur supporting his side of the family in the south? The Caw family may have come from around Arrochar, at the head of Loch Long. We do not

Glen Douglas

know the extent of their territory but, looking at subsequent boundaries, it seems likely that they were chiefs of the Lennox – the most northerly sept or sub-clan of Alt Clut. In medieval records, they are shown in Arrochar as a sept of the clan Macfarlane whose chief had the title the Mormaer (earl) of Lennox. So did the defeat of Caw by the Picts, and the probable decimation of his army mean the loss of the Lennox and a Pictish occupation?

The narrow neck of territory leading up to the Clach Nam Breatan reached into Pictish tribal territories in the north and marched with Dalriada in the west so it was the most vulnerable point of the Alt Clut frontier. Was this area the main focus of Arthur's early battles?

There are no further written clues but in the district of Lennox, local legend also has it that there was a battle in the neighbourhood of Duntocher and that Arthur's Stone at Strathblane is a memorial of one of his victories. This would account for the first five battles – first of all a battle to depose Caw and then a defensive campaign which recaptured lands taken by the Picts.

With the Scots providing auxiliaries for the Alt Clut

Dunadd as it might have appeared in the 7th century
Peter Dennis, Osprey Publishing

army, Arthur would have been in command of a formidable force. The arrangement suited them both and, unthreatened on their southeast flank, the Scots could concentrate their attention on developing their power base and expanding into the more sparsely populated territory of the Picts further north. The Britons and Scots continued to fight alongside each other in the years to come.

Alternative Sites

a) the Glazert Water to the north of Lennox Forrest on the frontier between Alt Clut and the Picts in the Campsie Hills where upstream there is still a place called Dunglass.

b) the muddy upper reaches of the Forth which later, in Gaelic, was called Abhainn Dubh (dark river) but, at the time, in old Welsh, the Firth of Forth was known as the Sea of Iudeu.

The Sixth Battle – A Fight For The Crown?

'The sixth battle was beyond the river called Bassus'

NENNIUS 8TH C

This is a difficult battle to locate. Apart from this one reference in Nennius' 8th century list, there is no other record of a river of this name. Place names including Bas are rare in the South of Scotland and the North of England. The place name could be derived from 'bas' meaning shallow and 'us' meaning water i.e. 'shallow water'.

In Alt Clut (Strathclyde), Cambuslang was the highest tidal bay on the Clyde. For a waterborne force it is a long way up river and to get there would have meant sailing in full view of the Alt Clut capital at Dumbarton – all very unlikely.

Rather than being an invasion, it seems more probable that this was another battle between rival Alt Clut factions. After his defeat by the Picts, Caw had been banished to a

monastic retreat in Wales. He was replaced as High Chief by Domnaguel, who ruled for seven or eight years before abdicating around 508–510 in favour of his son Clinoch and retiring to a monastery.

With the lands of Caw in the Lennox retaken, was the chieftainship now awarded to someone considered strong and able enough to hold it against future threats? Caw's eldest son Hueil and his younger brother were clearly hereditary claimants. Were they passed over? Disinherited, did Hueil and his brother feel there was nothing to lose in mounting a challenge perhaps not only for their traditional territory, but the High Chiefship as well? Was it Arthur, as the commander of the Alt Clut forces, who put down the rebellion? In any event, Hueil and his brother were killed in a battle and buried at Cambuslang. When their father died later in Wales, his body was brought back and he too was buried alongside them.

This is not the end of the story. Caw had another, younger son, Gildas, who, at the time of his father's banishment, had only been a small boy. With his mother, he had accompanied Caw to Wales where he grew up and was educated. He entered the priesthood and was ordained in Ireland. He returned to the lands of the Men of the North as a missionary for a time but finally ended his days in a monastery in Brittany where he died around 570.

He is remembered mainly for his book *De Excidio et Conquestu Britanniae* (The Overthrow and Conquest of Britain). Rhetoric was the core of Roman education and it is a critique of the depravity of a country falling apart through petty rivalries. Gildas criticises the destructive ambitions of continually fragmenting petty chiefdoms and the endemic corruption of the Church. It is based more on hearsay and oral sources rather than on historical documents but he relates events which occurred in his own lifetime. There are clear geographical inaccuracies and undoubtedly historical ones too. Writing in the period of peace and stability which came in the wake of Arthur's victories, he seems blissfully unaware of the impending threat of the Anglo-Saxon conquest that in the very near future, would sweep away his Celtic world.

Gildas was friendly with St Cadoc, the abbot of a Welsh monastery. Cadoc asked Gildas to act as locum while he travelled north on a missionary journey. In return, it seems that Gildas asked him to found a monastery over the graves of his father and brothers. This Cadoc did, building in stone at Cambuslang probably on the site of the present old Parish Kirk.

When he returned, both he and Gildas went into retreat as hermits on islands in the Bristol Channel – St Cadoc to Barry Island and Gildas to Flatholm where he wrote his history.

Gildas never mentions Arthur by name. He blames the misfortunes of his father and his family on Domnagual's son and successor, Clinoch. By the time he wrote his history, Arthur was long dead and had become immortalised as a national hero. As such, he was beyond criticism, so perhaps it was for the very personal reason of Arthur's involvement in the death of his brothers that Gildas could not bring himself to write his name.

In any event, Clinoch reigned for over 30 years. He was a popular ruler and a devout Christian. At much the same time, in Dalriada, Fergus's grandson acceded as High Chief of Scots and he too reigned for 31 years. Amazingly, after decades of constant warfare, neither chief fought a battle for the whole of their reigns. Peace came to the northern frontier and the Scots of Dalriada and the Britons of Alt Clut lived in harmony. Was this the political legacy of Arthur's military campaign?

Arthur is recorded as having had a strong presence at the Alt Clut capital Dumbarton – especially in the early part of Clinoch's reign. Both the Welsh Triads and a document dating from the time of David II of Scots confirm Arthur's presence there and even refer to it as 'Castri Arturi'.

By Gildas' time, Arthur had become not only a hero of the Britons but of the Scots as well. King Aedan mac Gabráin, crowned by St Columba in 573, named his eldest son Artuir – a name previously unknown in Gaelic. There are many place names in the Alt Clut area honouring Arthur. Whether they refer to this Scots Artuir who was killed in battle against the Angles before he could succeed to the throne or whether they refer to the original Brythonic Arthur it is impossible to say. However as well as Ben Arthur (the Cobbler) at the head of Loch Long, there is an Arthur's Seat in Dumbarton on the east side of the Leven, and Arthur's Face, a rock on the west side of Kinglas.

The Aln just above Bassington

Alternative Site

Bassington, ('ing' and 'ton' are teutonic suffixes) about three miles north west of Alnwick in Northumberland, lies by what today is known as the Eglingham Burn, a shallow tributary of the river Aln. Alnmouth with its sandy beach and sheltered harbour would have been an attractive landing place and a constant target for raiders. Later, in the Middle Ages, it developed into an important port. There was almost certainly a settlement where the Aln meets its tributary which the Venerable Bede called Adwifyrdi (at the two fords).

From 450 onwards, the Angles had been actively trying to colonise

Alnmouth

river valleys north of the Humber. But, as a landing site, it would have been equally attractive to Pictish raiders who travelled in fleets of small boats, each carrying 16 to 20 sailor warriors, relying mainly on oars but with sails as auxiliary power.

The Seventh and Eighth Battles – An Offensive?

The seventh battle was in the wood of Caledon, that is Cat Coit Caledon.

NENNIUS 8TH C

Cat Coit Caledon translates from the Brythonic as '*cad*' meaning 'battle', '*coit*' meaning 'wood' and '*Caledon*', the name of the forest which covered the whole of the country north of Hadrian's Wall. From the end of the 1st century to the beginning of the 6th there was a period of climate warming. The native oak, birch and hazel were in extensive regeneration and in Arthur's time, today's bare hills were densely forested, as indeed were the Central Lowlands of the Forth/Clyde valley.

The Caledonian Forest stretched right up into the Highlands. The earlier battles are all placed in relation to a specific river. Why is the location of this seventh battle so vague? Is it because it is in a part of the forest where there were no Brythonic place names – only Pictish? There

is therefore the intriguing possibility that after five victories against the Picts, in defence of the frontiers of Alt Clut, that Arthur could have now engaged in a punitive expedition into the Pictish homeland itself. Strategically, it would make sense to finish the campaign by putting the enemy's forward bases out of action and securing them as outposts of the Alt Clut. The Britons of the Alt Clut could thus control the approaches to Glen Falloch which seems to have been central to the earlier battles.

Dundurn Hill Fort today and as it might have been in the 6th century

From Loch Lomond, Glen Falloch leads north-eastwards and then the way splits, forking north to Loch Tay or south to Loch Earn. Both glens were an equal threat as a line of approach.

At the east end of Loch Earn lies the hillfort of **Dundurn**. It had probably been fortified since the Iron Age although the very limited excavations which have been carried out have only revealed defences dating back to about 600. Finds show that this was an important stronghold in the Dark Ages.

Atop a natural craggy pyramid of rock, it is a nuclear fort and would, in Arthur's day, have probably consisted of a wooden palisade round the top of the hill. At the western and highest part of the summit, a wide ledge has been cut out of the rock. This may have been to simply ease the timbered defences round an awkward corner. On the other hand, it is known as 'St Fillan's Chair'. It is in clear view from the floor of the glen and it might possibly have provided the coronation seat for the sub chiefs of Strathearn.

An impression of Dundurn in the 6th century
Peter Dennis, Osprey Publishing

Its position provides a bastion of the Southern Picts where a small force could control the passage from the west into Strathearn, and protect the fertile lands downstream from cattle rieving. Dundurn is however quite a way from the Pictish tribal capital round Forteviot. Indeed, the archaeological evidence suggests that Dundurn may have, at different times, been held alternatively by Picts, Scots and Britons.

By the 7th century it was the capital of a Pictish sub-chiefdom and Skene described it as 'an altogether exceptional work'. A path led to a gateway with double leaved gates with crossbars and surmounted by an entrance tower or walkway. It then wound its way clockwise up to the citadel. In military terms, the fort was a stronghold where dependants could gather while the main forces were away and into which cattle could be driven in the event of raids. As well as being a rallying point for defence, it also served as a storehouse and administrative centre.

When the High Chief was in residence, his retainers would include his bodyguard and household servants as well as specialists such as bards and craftsmen working bronze, iron, jet and glass. Excavations have revealed sixth century pottery from northern France which would almost certainly have been imported via the Clyde or Lorne. They also turned up a complete shoe with the leather decorated with an Irish (Scots?) design. It is unlikely that Dundurn could have been taken by force. If Arthur fought a battle and captured (or recaptured) and occupied Dundurn, it is more likely that it would have been a siege which forced a surrender, perhaps after a victory over reinforcements sent from the rear or maybe even as a result of a personal challenge – a fight between champions. Single combat played a large part in Pictish military encounters and, for example, a Pictish stone in Forres (Sueno's Stone) depicts two champions duelling with sword and buckler in front of a watching army. But strategically a victory here would be a job half done. To secure his lines, he would have had to retrace his steps to Glen Dochart and march north-east to Loch Tay, the possible site of the 8th battle.

Pictavia

Alternative Site

It has been suggested that the seventh battle was fought in the **Southern Uplands**, the old heartland of the Selgovae. The Selgovae are the most mysterious of the tribes of The Men of the North. We only know of them by the name the Romans gave them, meaning 'the hunters'. Remote in the forested uplands since their initial defeat by Agricola in the second century, they seem to have kept themselves to themselves – bottled up in their territory first by the Romans and then by the paid

A Traquair Bear – a folk memory of Selgovian times?

client chiefdoms of Alt Clut and Gododdin. By the end of the 5th century, after several hundred years of slow decline, they were out of step with their neighbours. During Roman times, they had benefited from trading – particularly skins and live animals. They had been one of the two major suppliers of bears for the arenas of Rome. However, the trade had dried up and, without the income to buy luxuries, their standard of living would have declined. They possibly then increased their cattle raiding and became an irritation to their neighbours. Men owed military service to their chief but petty rivalries between neighbours erupted easily and quickly and the country was constantly in a state of mini civil war.

Much of the Selgovae's original territory to the north in Lanarkshire and Peeblesshire and in the west in present day Dumfriesshire, seems by this time to have already been absorbed by Alt Clut and Gododdin. In the south, the area around Carlisle which had been Selgovian territory was incorporated into Rhegged (the western part of Coel's North Britain) and, in another generational subdividing, became the new chiefdom of Caer Guendolou. So their remaining territory seems to have consisted mainly of Selkirkshire and the western half of Roxburghshire.

Did a force of Alt Clut now attempt to further subdue the Selgovae and curb their raiding by incorporating the remnants of their territory and thereby pre-empting any further expansion northwards of Caer Guendolou? The Selgovae were still Pagan and the Druids had firm control, so any such operation would also have been a crusade against the infidel. The annexation certainly seems to have occurred during the reign of Domnaguel Hen of Alt Clut who, on his abdication in around 508/510, gave the Selgovae territory to his second son who is recorded as the first chief of a new chiefdom of Selcovia.

Moffat places the battle in the **Yarrow valley** where there is a standing stone with an inscription which 'marks the fatal battle of Prince Nudd of the Damnoni (Alt Clut). In this grave lie the two sons of Liberalis'. These two princes belonged to a branch of the royal family of Alt Clut who had the epithet 'liberalis', meaning generous. Their father Nudd was Chief of Selcovia. He was probably born in the 520s so to have two adult sons would place the battle in the 560s – say about 15 years after the fall of Dun Guyardi and the founding of the Angle Kingdom of Northumbria.

The stone was turned up by a plough in 1807/08 when the land

The Yarrow Valley

Above:
The Yarrow Stone with
its faint inscription

Middle:
The Glebe Stone

Right:
Warriors Rest

was being reclaimed for agriculture. It was then lying flat just under the surface and the remains of the princes' bones were underneath. All the evidence clearly points to a scene of slaughter here. Upstream from Yarrow Bridge is an area beside the river known as Dead Lake. Today, it is arable farmland but as recently as 1857 this was described as 'a marshy pool in the haugh' and, according to tradition, while the burials on the hill mark where the leaders fell, the bodies of the rank and file were thrown in here.

But it should also be remembered that only 25 years or so later, around 535AD, there was some kind of natural disaster like a volcanic ash cloud or a comet striking the earth which caused global climatic change, resulting in a collapse of temperature, a general failure of crops and the onset of the Yellow Plague which started in Persia and swept across Europe. Without carbon dating it is impossible to say for sure whether the bodies in Dead Lake would have been the victims of battle or of the pestilence which is said to have killed about a third of the population.

Yarrow Water running
through an area of natural
forest

The terrain is ideal for cavalry which would have been used by both sides. There were clearly heavy casualties. Geoffrey de Monmouth embellished history in his creation of the legend, but behind the fantasy are undoubtedly grains of truth. In writing about the Battle of Caledon he said:

The Catrail in the Cheviots marked by a V in the burnside and a line of dark green marsh grass

Arthur...ordered the trees round that part of the [Caledonian] wood to be cut down and their trunks to be placed in a circle so that every way out was barred to the enemy.

On the hillside overlooking the battlefield is a section of the Catrail which consists of a low rounded bank with a ditch. The ditch is rarely wider than 6–10 meters and the bank about four meters thick and half a meter above the bottom of the ditch. It runs in sections in a great curve for nearly 50 miles but is not continuous. It was clearly not a road, nor can it have been a defensive earthwork. The conclusion is that it was a monumental boundary marker and that wooden palisades may have filled the apparent gaps in the line. The traditional interpretation of the Catrail was as a political boundary created by the Angles after their victory at Degsastan in 603 but there now seems to be a consensus that it was probably built by Britons after the Roman withdrawal, quite possibly using the remains of an even earlier structure. Frontiers usually follow natural features such as lines of hills or rivers. In Southern Scotland, the geography is aligned east/west. So an artificial feature running north/south makes sense – a sort of 'no trespassing' line of demarcation, a symbol of power and dominance.

Behind Hadrian's Wall, the Romans had constructed a *vallum*, a ditch to demarcate the military zone and to keep civilians out. By the end of the Roman period, the Gododdin were extremely rich. Did they commission the building of the Catrail to mark the Selgovian boundary and keep them contained as the Romans had done? But, if so, why is the bank usually on the north or west side as this suggests that it is keeping the Gododdin out rather than the Selgovae in? Or was it

built later by Alt Clut after their incorporation of Selcovia? Until it is properly excavated, it will remain a matter of conjecture.

There are other similar dykes throughout Britain and Ireland such as Offa's Dyke in the Welsh Marches or the Devil's Dyke in Cambridgeshire and for a long time they were thought to be Anglo Saxon. However, recent archaeology in Cambridgeshire has revealed that the Anglo Saxons largely utilised older structures which can be dated back to pre-Roman Britain. Similarly, excavation of Offa's Dyke shows that it was built in the mid 5th century, a good 300 years before the Mercian king Offa after whom it is named. In Ireland, the Dorsey ramparts, which are like the Catrail. They run through South Armagh, were built around 100BC to mark the frontier of the powerful Kingdom of Ulster. The Dorsey also had gaps and the remains of a wooden palisade have been found in intervening bog land.

No matter when the Catrail was built, it positions the battle at Yarrow on the Selgovian frontier. In the place names along it, the prefix *cat* or *cad* (Battle) occurs locally at regular intervals (Cat-pair, Cat-ha, Caddonwe, Ca Craig, Catslack, Catlee, Cat Holes etc), suggesting a long history of frequent trouble.

This territory was certainly absorbed into Alt Clut and re-emerged as the new chiefdom of Selcovia. Did the annexation demand a major battle? Were the Selgovae capable of uniting as a tribal confederation? The indications are that they were constantly at war with each other and the terrain of thick forest did not favour a military invasion. Perhaps it was more easily absorbed piecemeal by a series of small campaigns, overcoming one sub-chiefdom after another over a period of time rather than by a single military invasion.

About six miles north of the Yarrow Valley, is Cademuir Hill where the Selgovae are said to have been defeated. As we have already discovered, Cad means 'battle'. In the Manor Valley on the north-west side of the hill there is a place called Arter's Brae and the victory according to local lore is attributed to Arthur. On the other hand, this was bear country and *Art*'s Brae could simply mean Bear's Brae. Cademuir rises to over 400 feet with commanding views of the surrounding countryside. It was clearly a major stronghold at one time with cultivation terraces and two forts. The largest of these contained over 40 huts. It appears to have been abandoned at the time of the Roman advance around 80AD and never reoccupied. The smaller fort which is protected by a *cheveux de fries* – a sort of tank trap of upright standing stones designed to slow down an attacking enemy – belongs to an earlier period. Like most archaeological sites, the hill has never been excavated, so there is no evidence whether it was still a settlement in the 6th century. However it is quite possible, indeed likely, that there was a decisive battle here which led to the Alt Clut occupation of Selgovian territory which included the Yarrow valley to the south

The Prince Nudd in the inscription was a son of the first Alt Clut chief of Selcovia, so he was certainly a generation after the incorporation of the territory. The chronology is too late for Arthur. The chiefdom was eventually lost to the Angles during the reign of Nudd's son. It would seem that this battle might not have been so much about the incorporation of Selcovia into the Alt Clut but more to do with the struggle to hold it against the Angles. As Moffat points out, only victors raise monuments so Nudd clearly won the battle and probably this was an Angle defeat in the latter part of the century.

> 'The eighth battle was in the stronghold of Guinnion in which Arthur carried a likeness of Holy Mary Everlasting Virgin on his shield and the heathens were turned to flight that day and there was great slaughter upon them'.
>
> NENNIUS 8TH C

Gwyn is Brythonic for 'white' so *Guinnion* (or *Gwynnion*) can be interpreted as the White Stronghold. At the foot of Loch Tay lies Fortingall. On the hill above the village is An Dun Geal. *Geal* is Gaelic for 'white' and *dun* is 'fort' – 'The White Fort'. It is in a strongly defensive position near the edge of a precipitous, rocky bluff, with good arable and grazing land in a high sheltered valley. The remains of a wall, 8 to 14 feet thick, still stands to a maximum height of four courses of massive stones. Originally, it is estimated that the walls would have been 12 to 15 feet high.

Dun Geal sits on top of the whitish rock face

Like Dundurn, it would have been a frontier outpost guarding the approach to Strathtay. The capital of this chiefdom of Atholl was at Logierait near the junction of the rivers Tay and Tummel. The chief owed allegiance to the High Chief of the Southern Picts in Forteviot who also ruled Fife, Forfar, Perth and Kinross – some of the richest land in Scotland. The tribe were wealthy, skilled traders. Between Logierait and Fortingall is a line of six, possibly eight, Pictish forts built on commanding heights with strategic views. They have unscalable crags to their front and were protected by walls and ditches to the rear. All are within easy walking distance of the farming settlements on the valley floor and many would have provided protection against cattle raiding.

But Dun Geal is a far stronger fortification than the chain of forts to the rear. All are within signalling distance of each other, providing the sub-chief in Logierait with a warning system so that an ever ready force of fighting men could be rapidly assembled. It is recorded that Dun Geal was the High Chief's own fort and, on this front line against attack from the Alt Clut Britons or the Gaels of Dalriada in the west, the High Chief could call out his immediate followers.

Left:
Dun Gael – the stone base of the ramparts

Right:
Dun Gael – rampart base at the entrance

We are told that 'Arthur carried the likeness of Holy Mary Everlasting Virgin on his shield and the heathens were turned to flight that day.' St Palladius is said to have set up a cell at nearby Aberfeldy in 469 and the number of dedications to St Mary in the surrounding area imply that it may also have been a St Mary shrine. The acceptance of the Virgin Mary as the Mother of God was established at the Council of Ephesus in 431 so the devotion to the Virgin Mary was a 'modern' cult and very much in vogue in the time of Arthur. But, with Aberfeldy established as a centre of a Christian mission 70 years earlier, were the enemy put to flight that day likely to be 'heathen'?

How established was Christianity? Palladius seems to have moved on to the Mearns after three or four years and so perhaps the new religion never took hold very deeply here. Had most of the people reverted to the old religion? Knowing perhaps of a small core of a Christian community in the Aberfeldy/Fortingall area, did Arthur deliberately ride with the likeness of the Virgin Mary to overawe the half Pagan Picts with a religious power of which they were already aware but, for the most part, had either not yet accepted or had allowed to lapse. And was he followed by new missionaries?

St Monenna and her maidens had moved up from Ayrshire to Dumbarton where their arrival seems to coincide with the peace which followed Arthur's early battles in the Lennox. It is interesting how closely St Monenna's progression mirrors that of Arthur. Did she follow him after the Battle of Guinnion and establish a mission at Loch Tay? Fortingall would have been reinforced by the other forts in the chain. With the defeat, it would seem likely that the neighbouring forts at Dull, Weem and Drummond Hill and perhaps even further down the glen would have been rendered indefensible. In which case,

The Fortingall community and church as it may have looked
Fortingall Community Council

Arthur would have controlled the whole area at the foot of Loch Tay.

Archaeology had identified a religious community at Fortingall with a number of artefacts from the 7th century but, in the summer of 2011, a new dig found what appears to be a 6th century bead.

At Inchadney, two miles downstream from Kenmore, there was a church (demolished in the 19th century) dedicated to the Nine Maidens, on a site dating back to the Arthurian period. In the 12th century, the nuns were granted a charter by King Alexander 1 in memory of his Queen Sybilla and they moved to Priory Island (originally known as the Island of the Holy Woman), a crannog in Loch Tay where Queen Sybilla had died in 1122. It remained in use until the Reformation.

The Nine Maidens
Well at Inchadney

Until quite recent times, the Nine Maidens were celebrated in an annual fair at Kenmore, known as the Holy Women's Fair. Remembering that the Picts were a matrilineal society, a group of women would have had a high status and perhaps more appeal and influence than a male community who might have been viewed as more of a threat and an intrusion. Glen Lyon is full of dedications to St Ninian and there are remains of several monastic communities dating back to at least the 7th century.

Whatever the truth, it is clear that there was an association with the Nine Maidens in the immediate area of Dun Gael.

After this eighth battle, there was a lasting peace with the Southern Picts. By neutralising their front line defences, did Arthur force them to sue for peace? Was the treaty then perhaps sealed by Arthur's second marriage – this time into a Pictish ruling family – to a bride named *Gwenhwyfar* (Guinevere)? This it must be said, while tantalising, is highly conjectural but I suggest deserves consideration. The basis for such a possibility is explained in the Twelfth Battle.

Alternative Sites for 'The White Fort':

a) **Whitcastle Fort** is in the Cheviots, not far from Hawick. It is so called because of the white sandstone. Not much of it remains because the centre has subsequently been quarried away but the circular earthen rampart is still visible.

b) It lies on the approach slopes of **Ruberslaw Fort** which, during the Antonine occupation, was the site of a Roman signal station. Ruberslaw is one of the most conspicuous landmarks in Roxburghshire – an isolated peak with magnificent views over the surrounding country. It seems that, after the Roman retreat, the dressed stone of the Roman buildings was reused to create a new citadel and a Gododdin lookout. It is about nine miles from the Catrail on the Selgovian border and is the only White Place that also appears to qualify as 'a strong place'. Ruberslaw could fit the bill. Was this the field of a final battle in the suppression of the remaining Selgovae in the south of their territory? On the hillside, just outside the ramparts, there is a St Mary's Well. With Nennius's reference to the Virgin, is this just coincidence?

Whitehill Fort with circular rampart and Ruberslaw on the summit behind

Gala Water

St Mary's Well near Stowe

c) Alistair Moffat and earlier writers such as Skene and Glennie indicate that Guinnion 'can suggest a holy place' and place this battle on **Gala Water**. There is an old hilltop fort north of Stowe which he suggests Arthur might have used as his base. Nearby there was a chapel and a healing well dedicated to Our Lady with an early Christian Mission and Sanctuary. But the battle was '**in** the stronghold of Guinnion' not **near** it, and a 'stronghold' is not a long abandoned hillfort being used as an overnight base. Anglian raiders at Stowe seem unlikely at this time but it could perhaps have been a battle against the last of the Selgovae.

d) Guinnion can of course also be connected to Uinniou (which, as explained earlier, is possibly the original spelling of Ninian).

The Significance of the Campaign

On balance, this eighth victory at the White Fort seems most likely the culmination of a campaign which neutralised the Pictish forward positions in the Southern Highlands and removed the threat of further invasion by the Southern Picts on the northern Briton frontier.

If this hypothesis is correct, Arthur had achieved something the Romans had never managed to do. He had subjugated the Southern Picts. If so, it was a superlative achievement and his reputation would have resonated to the farthest reaches of Celtic Britain and beyond.

This does not deny that, at much the same time there was a campaign which was probably piecemeal and did not need to involve Arthur to subjugate the Selgovae, incorporating them into Alt Clut. A similar takeover had already happened in the Galwyddel, in around 485. Thus the whole of the central and western half of present day Southern Scotland came under the overlordship of the Alt Clut.

In the tradition of his predecessors, Arthur recruited to his ranks the best of the warrior aristocrats of The Men of the North. Together they suppressed internal unrest and repelled any external threat. The reunification of Alt Clut with a strong High Chief had re-established a centre of power which was wealthier than the Gododdin and which could afford to subsidise the star treatment and quality training for the greatest heroes of the age.

The northern frontier was once again secure. But not so in South and Midland Britain where the Angles and the Saxons were consistently gaining ground.

The Ninth Battle –
An Alliance against the Angles?

'The ninth battle happened in the city of the Legion.'

NENNIUS 8TH C

There had been two 'cities of the legion' in Northern England – Chester and York. But Chester was abandoned 25 years before the final withdrawal. This left York (*Eboracum*), the city of the Roman sixth legion, the HQ of the *Dux Brittanicum* of North Britain and the centre of the road network.

Remains of the Roman city wall of York (Ebrauc)

After 410, the Latin *Eboracum* became the Celtic *Ebrauc* and the military zone became the high chiefdom of Coel Hen (Old King Cole) who had been the last *Dux Britannicum*. The capital remained in York but in succeeding generations, the territory was subdivided into separate chiefdoms.

By Arthur's time, the High Chief of Ebrauc was Coel's great grandson, Eilifer Gosgorddfawr. However the western half of the Roman military zone had been split off as a separate High Chiefdom and was ruled by Eilifer's cousin. This was now called Rhegged. In coalition, they had formed 'the Great Army' – an invincible force of spearmen.

Although the legions left Britain in 410, mercenary troops had stayed behind and, until as late as 436, Coel still commanded a force of professional Roman infantry who, with the collapse of the Empire, would have found it difficult to return to their lands of origin. On retirement, many of them had therefore been given land and settled locally. As they retired, they were replaced by local British recruits, so there was a continuity of Roman military tradition, standards and equipment. Old Welsh (Brythonic) had replaced Latin as the language of command but the 'invincible spearmen' were, in effect, Roman-trained infantry, just as the horsemen of the Manau Gododdin were the heirs of the Roman cavalry.

As 'conqueror of the Picts', was Arthur now asked to come south with his cavalry and take command of 'The Great Army' to lead an offensive to repel the advancing Angles? If so, he would have been at the head of a formidable force, every bit as effective and professional as the Roman army on which it was founded.

In 420, retired Anglian mercenaries, who had served in the Roman army, had been given settlers rights south of York around the upper reaches of the Humber. Originally, they had been recruited from around what is nowadays Schleswig Holstein on the Danish/German border – the Angle homeland. Ostensibly, they were subject to the chiefdom of Ebrauc but in reality they were semi-autonomous and they called their area Deira.

Angle immigrants had started settling in Norfolk at the beginning of the 5th century and, by Arthur's time, they ruled it as an independent territory. Around 480, they established a second kingdom in Lincolnshire known as Lindisfeorna (later Lindsey), a name which they subsequently transferred to their colony on Holy Island (Lindisfarne) in North Northumbria.

By the beginning of the 6th century, the Angles of Lindisfeorna (Lindsey) were looking to link up with their compatriots in Deira to expand across the Humber. Together they would then colonise northwards along the East Coast to link up with their footholds around the Tees, the Wear, the Tyne and eventually the Aln and Holy Island. With a

The site of the Roman ferry crossing of Dere Street to Petravia

steady flow of immigrants from across the North Sea, the Angle population was now growing every year in numbers and in strength. Within a few decades, Deira would indeed occupy all the land along the coast from the Humber up to Scarborough and Whitby.

On the north shore of the Humber were the ruins of Petravia, a Roman naval base and fort that had been abandoned around 370. This is where Ermine Street, the main road linking north and south, crossed the Humber with a ferry. If taken by the Angles, it would offer Deira freedom of movement to the coast and overseas. It would have been a major prize and was crucial to their colonisation of the east coast of Yorkshire.

The Humber at the site of the ferry crossing

Alternative Site

This battle may have been a few miles north of the city at **Catterick** where the road system forked north to Gododdin and west to Carlisle, Galwyddel and Alt Clut. If the Angles gained control of this key junction, they could rapidly deploy at short notice against any of the Northern chiefdoms. It was here that there was a final disastrous battle nearly a hundred years later which is the subject of a poem Y *Gododdin* and records the beginning of the end of the Men of the North. In one stanza, the author, Aneurin, praises the valour of a warrior called Gwawrddur:

> He fed black ravens on the ramparts of a fortress
> Though he was no Arthur
> Amongst the powerful ones in battle
> In the front rank. Gwawrddur was a palisade

Is this reference to Arthur because Arthur also fought here at an earlier time or is it just a reference to his bravery? Like Stowe, Catterick is a long way inland and the Angles were principally concerned in gaining a firm foothold on the coast. Would it not have been something of an impractical distraction to venture so far afield and try to hold their position?

The Tenth and Eleventh Battles – Angles or Picts?

'The tenth battle happened on the bank of a river which is called Tribruit'

NENNIUS 8TH C

'*Tri*' can be interpreted as 'ebb and '*Bruit*' can mean 'the speckled or multi-coloured strand'.

a) At **the mouth of the Humber,** on the north shore, the Romans had established saltpans. There are also archaeological remains of an Angle settlement here and a pagan graveyard has provided a wealth of artifacts dating from the first half of the 6th century.

> As the tyde comes in, yet bringeth a small wash seacole which is employed in the makings of salt..., an oylie sulpherousness being mixed with the Salts of the Sea as yet floweth...'.

This suggests a '*bruit*' – a multicoloured strand which would be most noticeable at low tide. Was this a second battle with the Angles? If the ninth battle secured the upper reaches of the Humber, it would be logical to also retake an Angle toehold in the lower reaches.

b) It has also been suggested that the definition of Tribruit – the multicoloured strand at ebb tide – might equally have applied to the saltpans on **the Forth** where there was the same combination with sea coal and this battle could just as well have been at the mouth of the river Avon in the Manau on the Firth of Forth. There is, of course, the Latin word *tributum*, meaning 'payment', and salt was a form of currency. And from the same Latin root is the 'tributary' of a river such as the Avon is to the Forth. Roman names survived, albeit in a slightly corrupted form.

Arthur may have settled the problem with the Southern Picts and peaceful relations were probably helped by the presence of missionaries fanning out into the territory from Culross and the Manau but in the north were the three tribes of the still pagan Northern Picts with a huge fleet of over a hundred boats with sails and oars, each carrying 16 to 20 men, who were able to raid wherever there was plunder.

Indeed, they had been the reason why Vortigern in South Britain had decided to bring in Saxon mercenaries after the Roman departure. But now, the Picts were faced with the serious presence of Angle and Saxon settlers and raiders in the South and the rich pickings were becoming less available. The Pictish tribes in the north were also becoming more united. Did they now look to raid closer to home?

The Picts were no strangers to the shores of the Men of the North. Throughout the Roman times they had always been on the horizon, with major attacks on Traprain Law recorded in 197 and 297AD and probably in the late 4th century as well. There were ports which were still important centres of trade. Was there a seaborne attack on the Lothian coast? If so, why now?

An invasion could have been provoked by an apparent weakness in the Gododdin defences. Lot had been succeeded by his son Gawain who was a largely absentee chief, spending much of his life in monasteries. Distanced from the policing and defence of his territory he immersed himself in religious pursuits – first in Galloway

A Pictish warship
Paul Wagner,
Osprey Publishing

(the land of his mother, Arthur's sister?), and then in Pembrokeshire where he eventually abdicated to take holy orders.

Without a strong presence, Gododdin appeared to have been becoming weaker, with increasing internal squabbles and fragmentation into sub-chiefdoms. Both Gododdin and Alt Clut had ports from which to trade, but the sea routes from France up the west coast were shorter and probably now safer than the North Sea. Thus there seems to have been a shift in favour of the Clyde and away from the Forth.

If Arthur was away with most of his troops fighting the Angles in the south, did the Northern Picts see this as a moment of opportunity to avenge the humiliation of their defeated southern cousins?

On the northern perimeter of Edinburgh airport is a standing stone known as The Cat Stone ('Battle Stone'). It is near the old Roman road to the old naval port at Cramond, beside the river Almond.

Although the stone originates from a much earlier period, it carries a Latin inscription added in the late fifth and early 6th century to mark the tomb of Vatta son (or daughter of Victus). Around it 51 Christian stone burial cists were discovered – all adults. Were they warriors slain in an unknown battle or perhaps victims of the plague such as that which swept the country around the time of Arthur's death? It was probably a later and maybe final battle between the Gododdin and the Angles of Nurthumbria but it remains a mystery.

'The eleventh battle is fought on a mountain which is called Agned' or in another copy of the manuscript ... 'on the mountain Breguion which is called Cat Bregion'.

NENNIUS 8TH C

Cat (battle) plus *brig* (high point) means 'battle on a high place'. Similarly, there is also an old Welsh word *agin* which also means 'high place'. Either way it seems to have been a battle on a mountain.

a) *Mynydd Agned* translates as the High Mount. But why does Nennius not use the Old Welsh name 'Dun Eidyn'? Is he waxing lyrical and referring to the castle rock or is he writing about Edinburgh's own '*mynydd*', an extinct volcano – now called Arthur's Seat. What was this called before it was Arthur's Seat? Was this *Mynydd Agned*? There are remains of hill terracing dating from Arthur's period and the remains of four Iron Age forts, two of which were probably still in use at this time. The ramparts of the fort situated between Arthur's Seat and Crow Hill are similar in construction to the later rampart at Traprain. The base of circular huts have also been found.

Traditionally, Holyrood Park has always provided grazing for the settlement on and around the castle rock. Even within recent memory, the cattle from the city's dairies in the Grassmarket were brought out daily to graze here.

Did the Gododdin cavalry graze their horses here? Twelve hundred years later, Bonnie Prince Charlie's army did and, interestingly, the poem *Y Gododdin*, which is said to have been written in Duddingston, the village at the foot of the southern slopes, speaks of:

> The rock of Lot's tribe,
> The folk of Lot's mountain stronghold at Gododdin's frontier;

It has also been suggested that, for the 'battle at Agned', there is an old Welsh word *agneaid* which means 'painted'. Similarly, for 'on the mountain of Bregion', there

Terracing on Arthurs Seat

Arthurs Seat

is *braith*, meaning mottled. Either could be a reference to tattooed Picts.

Geoffrey de Monmouth in 1137 was responsible for creating the legend of Arthur and the Knights of the Round Table, and located the battle at **Edinburgh.**

Alternative Site

b) **Another theory** is that the 'rocky high point' of the 11th battle may not have been Edinburgh. The name *Breguion* could have been the Old Welsh name for the Roman camp **Bremenium,** an important cavalry fort north of Hadrian's Wall on Dere Street.

The chiefdom of Bryneich, created by Coel Hen out of the southern part of Gododdin, seems to have been a weak link. It lacked the wealth and the resources of Gododdin in the north and of Ebrauc in the south. So it may have seemed a soft target to the Angles intent on colonising the mouths of the Tees, the Wear, the Tyne and Holy Island (Lindisfarne). Moffat suggests that, within the walls of Bremenium, Arthur could easily have concealed a squadron of cavalry in the stables.

Below the fort lies the river Rede and about a mile away is a crossing which, in Roman times, had a wooden bridge. By Arthur's time, it would have been reduced to a ford where men could cross waist deep. Arthur's long-range scouts would have reported the approach of an opposing force. Concealed in the woods, Arthur would have watched the enemy start to cross the river. Once they were split between the two banks, Arthur would have sounded the charge, outflanking the infantry before they could take a defensive position.

Remains of the Main Gate
Bremenium

But were the Angles the enemy? Bremenium is a long way inland and it seems that, at this time, the Angles were essentially interested in securing toeholds on the coast. The invasion inland would come a few decades later.

The Twelfth Battle –
The defeat of the Saxons

'The twelfth battle was at Badon Hill in which Arthur destroyed 960 men in a single charge on one day and no one rode down as many as himself'.

NENNIUS 8TH C

The sixth century monk, Gildas, (the younger son of Caw, the High Chief of Alt Clut who was defeated by the Picts and subsequently deposed) also writes of this battle but credits the victory to Ambrosias Aurelianus who was a generation older than Arthur. He too was a Christian and, according to the genealogies, may have been Arthur's uncle. He had spent his life campaigning in the south of Britain,

> that they might not be brought to utter destruction, [the Britons] took arms under the conduct of Ambrosias Aurelianus … Now in our times, our people are shamefully degenerated from the worthiness of their ancestors, who provoked to battle their

cruel conquerors, and by the goodness of the Lord obtained the victory. After this, sometimes our countrymen, sometimes the enemy won the field, to the end that our Lord might this land try after his accustomed manner these Israelites, whether they loved him or not, until the siege of Bath-hill [Baden] the last almost, though not the least, slaughter of our cruel foes…

In 457, Aurelianus had defeated Hengest at the Battle of Aylesford in Kent and over the next ten years took full control of British resistance in the south. Seemingly, his policy was containment rather than expulsion of Saxon settlements on the coast.

In 470, after the battle of Wallop in Hampshire, Ambrosias assumed the High Chiefship of Britain – in effect, a chief of chiefs. The Battle of Badon Hill was fought at the beginning of the 6th century but, by this time, Ambrosias was an old man. Nennius tells us that 'Arthur fought against these (the Saxons) in those days with the King of the Britons, but he himself was Leader of Battles'. So in other words,

From *Idyllis of the King* –
Gustav Doré

Ambrosias Aurelianus was present at the battle but Arthur was Commander in Chief.

Gildas does not mention Arthur by name but, as Gildas was the son of the deposed Caw, it may have been for family reasons that he could not bring himself to credit him directly. Alternatively, perhaps because everyone was so familiar with Arthur, Gildas simply took his presence as common knowledge.

The battle seems to have been a Saxon siege of a British hill fort in the South and the best contender for the site is, I believe, **Badbury Rings** near Wimborne in Dorset. At the time it was within ten miles of the Saxon front-line.

The Saxons first arrived in what was to become Wessex, around 495, when five ships landed somewhere on Southampton Water, perhaps at Calshot. With 30 men to a boat, this would represent a war band of about 150 men. Over the next few years, they consolidated their position and increased their numbers so that, around 508, they could engage in battle with the neighbouring British tribe and when, according to the Anglo Saxon Chronicle (which may well exaggerate numbers), they killed the chief and 5,000 Britons with him.

Over the next decade the Chronicle records two more major victories over the Britons. Winchester and Silchester were taken by the Saxons and Wessex, at this stage, covered an area to the boundaries of modern Hampshire. Then they turned their attention westwards towards Old Sarum (Dorchester) but they were checked by a major British victory. Was this Arthur's battle?

Badbury Rings from the east

The North Entrance through the ramparts and ditch

Badbury Rings was built during the Iron Age and dates back to about 800BC. Three concentric ramparts separated by deep ditches enclose a hilltop. It overlooks an important Roman crossroads where the road from Poole to Bath meets the road from Old Sarum (Dorchester) to Salisbury. The Anglo Saxons called it *Baddanbyrig. Byrig* (bury) is a Saxon suffix but *dan* is the same as the northern *dun* (fort).

Excavations suggest that the place was occupied right through the Roman period and continued into the fifth and perhaps sixth centuries. Originally, the ramparts were topped by a defensive wooden palisade. Whether or not this existed in Arthur's day, the steep ditches and 40 foot high ramparts would have represented a formidable defence and the height of the innermost rampart would have largely obscured any clear view of the men and horses within. The approach to the fort is a gently sloping chalk down – ideal for a cavalry charge.

The battle lasted three days and three nights. The Saxon army may have been lured forward by a small attacking force of local infantry who quickly broke and ran, luring the Saxons in pursuit. Concealed within the ramparts,

The Inner Rampart – the two figures show the scale. On top of the base was a wooden pallisade

it would have been difficult for the Saxons to assess the actual size of the force within. After three days, the Saxons would be running short of food and would have had to send out foraging parties thereby thinning their cordon. An unexpected charge at full tilt downhill would have broken the Saxon line and, once the Saxon wall was shattered, the real slaughter by the following wave of spearmen could have taken place.

Wherever the battle was fought, it seems that the Gododdin cavalry may have come south with the invincible spearmen of the Great Army of the North and, under Arthur's command, fought in coalition with the tribes of Southern Britain. Nennius also tells us that Arthur 'carried the cross of our Lord Jesus Christ… on his shield (shoulder)' – good religious propaganda which, as well as describing it as a fight for British survival, also makes it a fight for the Faith against the Pagans. Writing of the Battle of Catterick in 597, Aneurin also describes the Gododdin cavalry as carrying a white shield with a cross. It is interesting, however, that in the campaign against the Picts, who were fellow Celts with a recognised tribal territory, the battles were followed up by intense missionary activity to introduce a pan-tribal moral authority to help keep the peace. But, in the case of the Angles and Saxons, there appears to have been no acceptance of their territorial rights and no similar enthusiasm by the Celtic Church for missionary work. The Anglo Saxons were simply barbarians and intruders and it was not until 597 that the Roman Church sent St Augustin to start their conversion in Kent.

The *Annales Cumbriae* and a Gildas' account of the battle of Mons Badicus (Badon Hill) corroborate the Anglo Saxon Chronicle. Gildas writes that the battle of Badon Hill '… was (as I am sure) 44 years and one month after the landing of the Saxons and also the time of my own nativity'.

The Venerable Bede writing in 731 AD confirms that Ambrosius Aurelianus won a decisive battle over the Angles at the beginning of the sixth century. The Venerable Bede also records that Hengest and Horsa, the first Saxons, arrived in Britain in 449 AD. By adding this to Gildas' age, we arrive at a date of 493 AD. However, accurate dating is difficult because the early writers used different methods for dating Easter and this creates a possible variation of 25 years. The generally favoured date is 516AD.

Badon Hill was the successful conclusion to a campaign which had taken Arthur all over Britain. Archaeological evidence reveals that, after the battle, some of the Anglo Saxon settlements were actually abandoned, their frontiers were pushed back and some communities even gave up entirely and returned to the continent. Interestingly, the Anglo Saxon Chronicle records a second battle at 'Beranbury' 40 years later (556) but does not claim a Saxon victory.

Alternative Site

Another suggestion is the steep-sided **Solsbury Hill** above the village of Batheaston in the Cotswolds. The suggestion is that a British retreat would have lured the Saxons deep into British territory, stretching their lines of communication. But Solsbury is about a hundred miles from the then Saxon frontier and archaeological excavation of the site has shown no evidence of occupation after the arrival of the Romans in the first century. The Saxons do not appear to have reached this far west much before the fall of Bath in 577. The notion that the battle was fought near Bath was first mooted by Geoffrey de Monmouth in his 12th century best seller. But as explained later in the story of the legend, de Monmouth transposed the locations to Cornwall and the South West for political reasons. He therefore holds little credibility as a source.

There is, however, also a school of thought that, in fact, Arthur's battles were all north of the Wall and that Badon Hill could be against a sea born invasion by the Northern Picts at **Bowden Hill** on the borders of the Manau Gododdin in what today is West Lothian but this ignores the ease of mobility which the old Roman roads gave Arthur to deploy rapidly from one end of Britain to the other.

Solsbury Hill

Summary

The sites of the 12 battles of Arthur's campaign and the enemy forces are highly speculative. Only archaeological research can prove or disprove the suppositions above but below is a summary of the possibilities.

No	Place Name	Chiefdom	Probable Location	Enemy
1	Glein	Alt Clut	Lennox or Ayrshire	Civil War or S. Picts
2	Linnius	Alt Clut	Lennox	S. Picts
3	Linnius	Alt Clut	Lennox	S. Picts
4	Linnius	Alt Clut	Lennox	S. Picts
5	Linnius	Alt Clut	Lennox	S. Picts
6	Bassus	Alt Clut	Cambuslang	Civil War
7	Caledon	S. Picts or Selgovia	Strathearn	S. Picts
8	Guinnion	S. Picts or Selgovia	Strathtay	S. Picts
9	City of the Legion	Ebrauc	Yorkshire	Angles
10	Tibruit	Ebrauc/ Manau	Yorkshire or W. Lothian	Angles or N. Picts
11	Agned or Breguion	Gododdin or Bryneich	Lothian or Northumberland	N. Picts Angles
12	Badon Hill	S. Britain	Dorset	Saxons

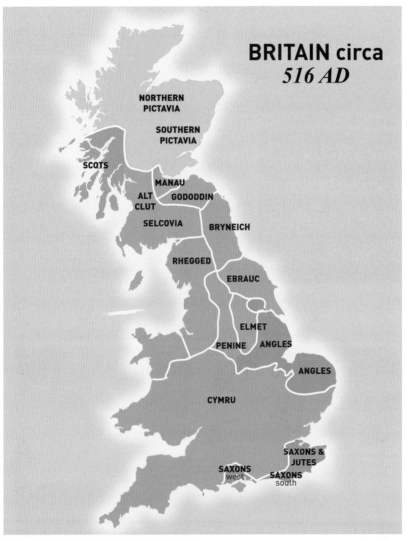

BRITAIN circa
516 AD

NORTHERN
PICTAVIA

SOUTHERN
PICTAVIA

SCOTS

MANAU

ALT
CLUT

GODODDIN

SELCOVIA

BRYNEICH

RHEGGED

EBRAUC

ELMET

PENINE

ANGLES

ANGLES

CYMRU

SAXONS &
JUTES

SAXONS
west

SAXONS
south

Arno Vilanove

The Arthurian Peace
516–537

From *Idyllis of the King* –
Gustav Doré

Stirling – Castle Rock,
the capital of Manau

Britain now entered a period of stability and Arthur could live peacefully in Manau. In any of the other British chiefdoms, Arthur and his cavalry were there as guests but Manau was home turf where Arthur governed alone. Ever since circa 370, when Padarn Beisrudd ap Tegid (Padarn of the Scarlet Cloak) was sent north as the first Preafectus Gentium of Manau, the cavalry HQ had been near the front line at Stirling. It was the gateway to the heartlands of the Southern Picts. Whoever held Stirling controlled the passage of people and goods between north and south.

Archaeological evidence has revealed two Dark Age forts at Stirling, one on the Castle Rock and another on Abbey Craig on the north side of the river (where the Wallace Monument now stands). Presumably Abbey

Abbey Craig

Craig was a forward position. It was within easy signalling distance of the Castle Rock and with an uninterrupted view of the Ochils.

Excavations have uncovered stone ramparts framed with timber and lined with flat flagstones for lookout patrols. They also found two gateways.

The site actually dates back to the Iron Age but a citadel was in use here around the time of Arthur until around 780. The strategic value of the site was highlighted several centuries later when William Wallace lay in hiding, waiting for the invading army of Edward I of England to cross the river. When they were half way across, Wallace and his

Base of the Abbey Craig rampart

Castle Rock from
Abbey Craig

cavalry broke cover to route an enemy force many times larger than their own.

Like any other chief, Arthur would have moved around his settlements in Manau. Conditions at the windblown fort on the hill would have been Spartan and with the threat of attack now considerably reduced, Arthur may have preferred a more comfortable life on the plain. Fifteen miles downriver from Stirling, the Forth is joined by its tributary, the Carron. This is near the eastern end of the old Antonine Wall and, during their occupation, the Romans had built an important fort here. The Latin name was Colonia. It consisted of a North Fort which covered six acres and seems to have housed the military garrison. Alongside it, a South Fort provided a defended settlement for traders and families. It was built to guard the crossing of the military road over the river Carron. At that time, the river was navigable and served as a supply port for men and materials to the Wall.

In the centuries which followed, it developed into an emporium for a major trade route to the north and it was probably rebuilt by the Romans in the 380s. Today, the place is called Camelon and is the site of Falkirk Golf Course. The remains of the fort were still visible in the late 18th century and until the 19th century it was actually called Camelot but we do not know what it was called in Arthur's day.

Camelon in the 19th century
Falkirk Local History Society

In the time of Arthur, international merchant ships arrived in the Firth of Forth at the old Roman naval base at Cramond, as well as Leith, Rosyth and Largo, often also putting in at Berwick and Gullane on the way. Some even ventured further north to the Tay and to Forres on the Moray coast. The Forth was navigable as far as Stirling but it was a meandering course up-river. Camelon was closer to open water where a

The Roman fort of Colonia was sited on top of the hill at what today is Falkirk Golf Course

vessel could quickly get under sail and it would have been an important entrepot for Manau.

So did Arthur base himself for a time at Camelon, where, with all its little imported luxuries he could indulge Guinevere, his second and much younger wife, and fete his court in the annual round of feasting and hunting?

The Celts are recorded as being immoderate in their love of food and intoxicating drink. There were, however, strict rules of custom and tradition which also had to be followed. Restraint, a sense of honour and clever conversation were all virtues to be valued. The bards would sing, recite poems and

View from the site of Camelon Fort towards the distant Ochils

tell tales celebrating the ancestry, courage and generosity of the hosts and satirising those they disliked. Music would be provided by the lyre, the harp, the drum and the flute and there would be dancing. Feasting took place on the many Christian holy days and around the traditional pagan seasonal festivals which did not die out but merely adopted a Christian significance.

There were four important seasonal festivals. The pagan god, Bel, was the sun. *Beltane*, on the first of May, marked the beginning of summer when the livestock have had their young and the sun is rising in the sky. Immediately before the transhumance migration to summer pastures, it was a time of ritual cleansing. As the sun rose, people would gather at the highest point to wash their faces in the dew. Fires were lit and livestock were driven through a passage of flames to cleanse and protect them from misfortune. People danced clockwise in a circle and made special sun-shaped oatmeal bannocks. In earlier times, on each bannock were nine square knobs, each symbolising a different totem. The people would break off a knob and throw it over their shoulder as an offering to a particular totem, saying for example 'This I give thee O Fox, spare my lambs'.

The traditional hillforts were the sites for these annual festivals and a place where animals were bartered. With the advent of Christianity, we do not know the detail of how these earlier customs were adapted but even today in Edinburgh, on May Day, people climb Arthur's Seat to wash their faces in the dew at sunrise.

Lughnasadh on 1 August was the date for the start of hand fasting or 'bundling' – trial marriages where a couple could live together for a year. At the end of the period, they either had to marry or separate – but separation held no stigma. Lugh was the greatest of the Celtic male gods. He was master of many arts, a god of light and genius.

Samhain on the 1 November was the end of transhumance (now Halloween or All Saints). This was the end of the Celtic year. Surplus beasts were slaughtered to be dried or salted for the winter, and, in pagan times, there were rituals where the ancestors were invoked to keep away evil and misfortune. It was a time when the barriers between the worlds of the living and the dead were at their weakest and there was free movement of the dead to revisit their old haunts. Bonfires played an important role in purification rituals. The dead lived in a realm of joy and delight, a land of eternal youth where the feasting and drinking never came to an end. Death was only a transitional event in the course of life. The Celts had no concept of hell. This was a Christian innovation. If one led a really bad life then you simply were not accepted into the world of the ancestors and you ceased to exist. The ability to see and speak with ghosts still remains within the bounds of normality in Celtic countries, as does the gift of second sight and déjà vu.

Imbolc (which corresponds to Candlemas) on the 1 February was a time of fertility and rebirth. Bonfires which symbolised the power of the sun produced ash which people rubbed on their faces for good luck and for disguise. This 'guizing' (disguising) symbolically prevented partners from recognising each other and a certain amount of promiscuity was allowed. Men dressed as women. Women dressed as men (possibly the Roman Saturnalia evolved from these earlier Celtic customs). The days were growing longer. The sap was rising. It was the beginning of new life after the hibernation and dark days of winter. It was the Rite of Spring – fire out of darkness.

For a good 20 years, following the Battle of Badon in 516, Arthur and Guinevere enjoyed a life of peace and plenty. But eventually the idyll was shattered. There is a record of one final battle in 537AD – against whom we are not sure but Nennius says that 'in the strife of Camlann… Arthur and Medraut perished'.

Medraut was a younger son of Lot and Arthur's sister. In the tradition of 'fostering', the boy had been apprenticed to his uncle, Arthur, to learn the skills of horsemanship and warriorhood. He would have fought alongside Arthur in his later battles and had earned a reputation as a skilled and mighty warrior. But Nennius' words are ambiguous. Were Arthur and Medraut fighting on the same side or were they on opposing sides at the battle of Camlann? And what were they fighting about? In either case, the outcome was that Medraut was killed and Arthur mortally wounded.

K. Halleswelle

If Arthur and Medraut were fighting together on the same side, this would seem perfectly logical as Arthur was now an old man and, while remaining the commander in chief, he would need a younger man to lead the cavalry. Who better than the nephew he had trained? It would have been a similar relationship to that of Arthur and Ambrosias Aurelianus 20 years earlier at Badon Hill. Camelon would have promised rich pickings for a raider out for plunder but for 20 years before the battle there is no record of any raids. Furthermore, the peace between the Picts and Britons seems to have held long after Arthur's death. The battle therefore appears to have been an isolated incident.

The apparent lack of any follow-up (which one would expect of an enemy wishing to capitalise on the weakness and disarray caused by Arthur's death) seems to bring us back to the conclusion that it was indeed a fight between Arthur and his nephew. If this was the case, Medraut had his own cavalry. Remember that the Romans had not only established the force in Manau but also in the tribal territories and that the Gododdin had their own cavalry which continued from the late Roman times right through to the defeat by the Angles at Catterick in 597AD.

As a place name, Camas is a prefix which indicates a bay or a beach where ships can be drawn up out of the water. A combination with the name of the Gododdin Lot would be Camaslot or Camalot (Lot's Landing). But in all the historical Arthurian material the name is absent and Camelot only appears for the first time in the 12th century French romances. Most modern scholars regard Camelot as being entirely fictional. But was it?

Geoffrey de Monmouth was the first to seriously enhance the fairly scant historical facts to make a better story. In 1137, he wrote his *Historia Regum Britanniae* in which he describes Arthur as a great Celtic warrior king, unsurpassed in prowess and political diplomacy but the idea of placing Arthur and Medraut on opposing sides first occurs in *The Mabinogion* (of which the surviving copies only date from the late 14th century – two centuries after Geoffrey de Monmouth). The Mabinogion is a somewhat random collection of early Welsh songs and stories in which Arthur features rather inconsistently. The stories had, by this time, been developed, elaborated and handed down over several centuries and the old British chiefdoms of the Men of the North had long since disappeared.

When the Gododdin finally fell to the Angles in 670, their records were moved for safekeeping to Dumbarton in Alt Clut. Two hundred years later, in around 890, Alt Clut, in its turn, fell to the Vikings and the surviving documents were carried by ship to Wales – the last stronghold of the Old Welsh (Brythonic) language and culture. By the time of Geoffrey de Monmouth, Old Welsh had all but died out in what had by now become Scotland. The name 'Y Goggled' (the Men of the North) had been transposed from the lost territories north of the Wall to North Wales (Gwynedd) and in Welsh legend Arthur had been adopted as a Welshman. But in Scotland, he was not forgotten. A mile or so downriver from Camelon, there was a Roman building known as Arthur's O'en, described by a Flemish cleric in 1120 as 'a palace of the warrior Arthur... In which the history of all his exploits and wars is to be seen in sculpture'.

Top:
Arthur's
O'en before
demolition

Above:
Arthur's O'en
18th century
replica at
Penicuik House

This is 17 years before Geoffrey de Monmouth wrote his legend and indicates that, although all the Gododdin records had been shipped to Wales, Arthur was still remembered north of the Wall. Arthur's O'en is mentioned again in 1293 as *fumum Arthur* – presumably because of its round oven shape. The building was unique in Britain and is believed to have originally been a victory monument, clearly visible from the Antonine Wall, to commemorate the campaign of Lollius Urbicus which preceded the Wall's construction. By Arthur's time it was already 350 years old. Did it simply get its name because Arthur fought a battle here?

If Camelon is indeed the site of the battle of Camlann then Arthur almost certainly knew the building.

Did he use it before the battle or was he perhaps brought here afterwards to rest and bathe his wounds?

Today, nothing remains. The building was demolished for its stone in 1743 but, at the same time as its destruction, an exact replica was built at Penicuik House in Midlothian.

Inevitably, of course, it has been suggested that this building housed the Round Table, an artefact which is first mentioned in a Norman French manuscript by Robert Wace in 1155. We will never know whether or not Arthur had a special round table but he almost certainly ate in the round. Feasting was a celebration of Celtic life and social unity. Hospitality was important. A stranger was not asked his business until he had eaten his fill. Atheneus, writing at the beginning of the third century, records that 'when a large number dine together, they sit around in a circle with the

most influential man in the centre... whether he surpasses the others in warlike skill, or nobility of family, or wealth.'

The legendary Knights of the Round Table were the creation of medieval poetic license but Arthur's cavalry were all drawn from the cream of the warrior aristocracy – in medieval terminology they would have been called 'knights'!

There are several medieval references to the 'tabyll round' being kept at Stirling. These clearly derive from Monmouth's account and later versions of the legend. In the former royal gardens situated in the park below Stirling Castle, there is a geometrical earthwork, constructed in the 1620s for Charles I, which is known as the Kings Knot. A geophysical survey in 2011 revealed the existence of the circular ditch and mound of a more ancient feature which served as the base for the Knot. One suggestion is that it is a burial mound. Could this be the last resting place of Arthur? This is highly unlikely but only excavation can uncover the truth.

Guinevere is recorded as Arthur's second wife, thereby implying she might have been considerably younger than him. By this time, Arthur would be approaching three score and ten. In the Triads of the Isle of Britain there is a list of the three unfaithful wives of Britain which ends 'and one was more faithless than those three: Guinevere, wife of Arthur, since she shamed a better man than any of them'. Married to a much older man, was Guinevere unfaithful with Arthur's nephew Medraut who would have been about forty and more of her own age? In the *The Mabinogion*, a poem, 'The Dream of Rhonabwy', describes how the quarrel between Medraut and his uncle was caused by a falling-out between Guinevere and her sister Gwenhwyfach. 'Gwenhwyfach struck upon Gwenhwyfar (Guinevere) and for that cause there took place afterwards the Action of the Battle of Camlann'.

Why did Gwenhwyfach give the game away? It has been suggested that perhaps she had a relationship with or was married to Mordred and so was also betrayed.

In a culture governed by ties of kinship, breaching those obligations was to destroy the basic structure of society. It caused strife. It killed a whole network of relationships and so was viewed on a par with murder – the worst possible crime.

Did Arthur condemn Guinevere to death for her adultery and did Medraut try to abduct her? Or is *The Dream of Rhonabwy* simply a medieval romance adapted to follow the popularity of Geoffrey of Monmouth's account?

Curiously, Arthur's name is still remembered in the very heart of the Southern Picts. In Angus, around Blairgowrie and Couper, there is a collection of Arthur place-names within a small area – Arthur's Stone, Arthur's Seat and an Arthur's Fold. It would have been logical, after his victories against the Southern Picts, for Arthur to have sealed the ensuing peace treaty with a marriage. There is an old nursury rhyme –

> *Frae Perth came Guinevere,*
> *To make the King revere,*
> *He saw her face in the Loch of the north,*
>   *And never went more forth*

Boece, the 16th century Scottish historian, relates that, once discovered, Guinevere fled back across the Pictish frontier to her own people, knowing that, in Manau, she would be condemned to death for her infidelity.

From *Idyllis of the King* –
Gustav Doré

Was she abducted by Mordred before he confronted
Arthur? Did he perhaps provide a passage on a ship? By
sea, Guinevere would have been safer from pursuit. Just
outside Alyth is Barry Hill, the site of an Iron Age hillfort.
Local lore recounts that Guinevere was brought here. The
fort is believed to belong to different periods but until it is
excavated, we will not know for sure whether or not it was
still in use in the early part of the 6th century.

Guinevere is referred to as 'the wanderer' (perhaps as
much in a moral sense as geographical!). In Pictish, her
name was Vanora (or Ganore). This has the same meaning
– 'the fair one' or 'the white lady' (literally, 'white wave').

It seems that the local people had no sympathy with
her immorality. She had brought shame on her people. In
Meigle Churchyard, there is a mound which is reputed to
be her grave and in the museum there is a carved Pictish
stone which stood here. According to local legend, it depicts

Barry Hill by Alyth

Vanora (Guinevere) being torn to pieces by wild beasts, although it is more probably a representation of Daniel in the Wilderness being befriended by wild animals.

One can only take the story with a pinch of salt but it is interesting to find an Arthurian tradition in the heartland of one of the four tribes of the Southern Picts. South of the Highland Line, the culture and language of the Britons was eradicated by invasion. But in Angus, the Pictish culture merged with the Scots and, while the Pictish language was lost, Pictish lore was not. So perhaps it is not unreasonable to wonder if there is not a glimmer of fire behind the smoke?

Not only are Arthur and Guinevere remembered in the area but, once again, there is also a presence of the Nine Maidens. *The Life of St Monenna* says that the Nine Maidens moved from Dumbarton to Stirling (*'in Castello quod dictur Strevelin'*). Later, St Monenna founded a

Daniel and the lions or Vanora (Guinevere) being killed by wild animals?

chapel on the castle rock in Dun Eidyn (Edinburgh) which became referred to as '*Castra Puellarum*' – the Castle of the Maidens, a name which was in use until very recent times and to which Geoffrey de Monmouth refers in locating Arthur's 11th battle. At Edinburgh, she left five of her 'maidens' to form a

community. An excavation close
to St Margaret's Chapel on the
Castle Rock in 1835 unearthed
a number of female bodies and
several coffins.

Monenna then founded
another religious settlement at
Dunpender (*Mons Dunpeledur* –
Traprain Law), the old Gododdin
capital, where archaeology has

Vanora's Mound Meigle
Kirkyard

since revealed the foundations of an early church in the
centre of the hillfort. Finally, it seems, she established a
mission to the Southern Picts and spent the remainder of her
days at Longforgan, on the north bank of the Tay, five miles
west of Dundee where she died circa 518AD (the Ninewells
district of Dundee is thought to be connected either with
the Nine Maidens or with Ninian). Again, it is suggested
that *The Life of St Monenna* in Scotland might not really
be about the Irish St Monenna from Ireland but is another
distorted remnant of the life of St Ninian (mis-transcribed
as Mo-Uinn or Mo-Ninn or in Gaelic Mo-Finn).

In either case, by 530, the Christian community at
Longforgan would have been well established with out-
stations further inland. Within a 20 mile radius of Alyth,
the Nine Maidens are remembered in the names of wells
at Glamis and at Cortachy, near Forfar, where it is believed
that before the Reformation there was also an altar to the
Nine Maidens in the church. There was another altar to
them at Finavon. A chapel and burial ground at Alyth were
dedicated to St Ninian.

It is also clear that there had been a strong missionary
presence at Stirling long before Arthur's arrival. In the later
abbey there was a St Ninian altar and on the site is a St
Ninian spring where there was a chapel and which, in the
12th century, gave its name to the parish. There was also a St
Ninian altar in Stirling Parish Church and a St Ninian Well
near the South Port. South of Stirling, on the Roman road
from Camlon, is the old church of Eccles (Latin 'ecclesia')
which later became St Ninians old parish church.

So, in Arthur's day, there would have been a well-

The river Carron – three miles downriver from Camelon

established Christian community at Eccles. The parish at that time was much bigger than it is today and included the parishes of Gargunnock, Denny and Dunipace, Larbert, and probably Bothkennar and Airth. This would have been the core of old Manau but Manau would by now have included modern Clackmannan, possibly some of Mentieth, and the Falkirk area as far as the Avon.

The church of Eccles was the place where the dead near Stirling were taken for burial. This is also confirmed around 1140 by the charters of Alexander and David for the foundation of Cambuskenneth Abbey when they had to clarify where people living on crown land, parish land or the burgh were to buried when they died and to which church the important burial revenue went. Until Alexander founded his new church in the castle, everyone (apart from the burgesses who were buried at Holy Rood) was buried at Eccles. When St Monenna herself died, it is written that her own body was brought here.

The buildings of the early Celtic monastery would have been humble. The church would have been a timber-framed, wattle and daub hall with a thatched roof and set on stone foundations. The altar would have been on a paved area and the window slits high and narrow. An encircling bank and ditch to keep out wild animals and marauders would

Arthur on the barge to Avalon
Robert Hope

have been enclosed by circular monastic cells of turf or dry stone with thatched roofs. There would probably also have been a mill for grinding flour, a brewery, a wash place and latrines. The infirmary would have been alongside the church, as would have been the refectory, kitchen, stores and possibly a scriptorium.

The daily routine was ordered

The River Forth below Stirling

by the ringing of heavy hand bells like the one still in the church at Fortingall (illustrated on page 48). Married men were admitted to the priesthood and nuns had equal status with monks. Each would have had their own separate cell. Their life was simple and based on contempt for worldly goods. They ate and assembled for chapel together but there was considerable freedom of movement. Apart from being priests and missionaries, they were also doctors, farmers and builders. The monastery would have contributed to provisioning Arthur's cavalry.

In Geoffrey de Monmouth's 12th century *Life of Merlin*, he introduces a character called Morgan le Fay, supposedly Arthur's half sister. She is the leader of the 'nine maidens of Avalon' who took Arthur away on a barge after the Battle of Camlann. In the early stories she is presented as a healer and as a

The graveyard at Eccles (St Ninians). Was this the last resting place of Arthur?

Cambuskenneth Abbey from the river

benevolent presence. Is she perhaps based on Monenna or one of her maidens?

Eccles would have been a place of healing and a centre of medical excellence. Carried upstream on a flood tide, Arthur could have been brought here where his wounds would have been tended under the best possible conditions. It was also a place where he could have received the last rites and is almost certainly where he would have been buried.

As for the name, 'Avalon,' it was probably 'borrowed' to make a better story from a place in France which Geoffrey de Monmouth would have known about from his Breton origins and of which more later in the story of the growth of the legend.

The Isle of Avalon means 'the Isle of Apples'. The name could derive from the Old Welsh word for apple, *afal*. Apples were introduced into Britain by the Romans and, for centuries, Stirling was famous for its apple orchards. The later abbey of Cambuskenneth, only one and a half miles from Eccles, was surrounded by orchards which, were only cut down as recently as the 1950s to make way for housing. So it is perfectly conceivable that earlier there may have been orchards on the Stirling side of the river as well. There could also have been a religious community at Cambuskenneth before the building of the 12th century Abbey. Although the site has never been excavated, the remains of what appears to have been a Celtic cross were discovered in a village garden next to the Abbey. In Old Welsh, *Abh* (pronounced 'av') means river and *Lann* is 'church'. But maybe the apples, like Avalon, are just an element of poetic license.

It is recorded that Arthur had three sons by his first wife but they all predeceased him. After his death, the succession to Manau passed to a landless younger brother of Clinoch, High Chief of Alt Clut, called Cunbelin Map Dumnagual.

Exploiting the prolonged absence of the Gododdin's religiously inclined High Chief, Gawain, in Wales, Cunbelin annexed some Gododdin territory in the Lothians and created a new sub-chiefdom calling himself Chief of Dun Eidyn with his younger brother, Brychan, as Chieftain of Manau.

Manau lasted until the 7th century before falling to the Angles of Northumbria. The last reference is a battle on the Plain of Manau (between the Avon and Carron) in 711AD.

Alternative Sites

The Allan Water joins the Forth just upriver from Cambuskenneth. Was Camelon perhaps Camallan? This seems highly speculative.

The Isle of May, at the mouth of the Forth, is suggested by Stuart MacHardy as possibly deriving its name from the Isle of Maidens. Burials on the site of the church have been radiocarbon dated at least to the seventh century but there are probably earlier remains. However, it is a wind swept place and certainly an unlikely spot for apple orchards – if apples have anything to do with it.

Camboglanna (Castlesteads) is the 12th fort from the east on Hadrian's Wall. It is not far from Carlisle and the Solway which is the second most powerful tidal estuary in Britain. On an ebb tide, a barge might have carried the wounded Arthur down to the abbey on the Isle of Whithorn. For over 100 years, Whithorn had been renowned as a pilgrimage centre of healing and miracles and a burial place for saints and heroes. But it is a long way downriver – nearly 60 miles (100km). The Galloway Pippen (*Croft-en-Reich*) was introduced into Wigtonshire by the Romans. It is also interesting to note that at

The Solway

the end of Hadrian's Wall on the south shore of the Solway is a fort which the Romans built to guard against raids by the Novantae and Selgovae who occupied the northern shore. They called it Aballava. (meaning 'orchard') and in the seventh century *Ravenna Chronology* it is called Avalana.

Engraving on the lead cross in the tomb in Glastonbury

At **Glastonbury** in Somerset, 50 years after the publication of Geoffrey de Monmouth's *Historia*, the monks conveniently discovered Arthur's tomb! An account in 1190 records 'I have seen the cross and retraced the letters sculpted on it "here lies buried the famous king Arthur and Guinevere, his second wife on the island of Avalon'. Ever with an eye to boosting the pilgrimage business, the exhumation was almost certainly a publicity stunt. With a monarchy trying to promote an English national identity, the timing was politically correct. Also Glastonbury was faced with a major rebuilding programme after a disastrous fire. Why would the bones be shipped south when the monks of Whithorn seem to have reached an agreement with the Vikings and were left unmolested? It seems highly unlikely. The cross disappeared sometime during the 18th century but an engraving of it still exists.

Roxburgh or Marchidun (Fort of the Horsemen) is another alternative. Alastair Moffat suggests that it is a possible candidate for Camelot. The motte is very steep and may have been reinforced by what appears to have been a dry moat. It could easily be held by a squadron of 300 men. Sitting on a narrow neck between the rivers Tweed and Teviot, just before they join, it is a superb site for a stronghold. The haugh below the fort is large enough to grow several crops of hay and to graze a breeding herd all the year round. It was almost certainly in use at the time and it is perfectly positioned to both defend the southern frontier of the Gododdin and to police the Selgovian frontier to the west.

The Gododdin would have had numerous cavalry bases in different parts of the country. It is perfectly reasonable that this would indeed have been a cavalry fort and was certainly the seat of a Gododdin chieftain who was responsible for the defence of the Gododdin's southern frontiers with Bryneich and Selgovia. But it seems unlikely to have been Arthur's HQ or Camelot.

About five years after Arthur's death, the Angles took Dun Guayardi, the capital of Bryneich, followed rapidly by control of the coastal area up to the Tweed. Bryneich continued to exist for another 60 years or so but was reduced to the interior, western half of the original territory. In this period, Marchidun would have assumed considerable importance and could well have been the Gododdin military HQ for the defence of their southern frontier.

A century after Arthur, it too fell into Angle hands and became a base from which the Angles launched offensives against Alt Clut and their sub-chiefdom of Selcovia (e.g. the battle of Yarrow). The site continued to be important throughout the Angle occupation and, in medieval times, grew into the third most important city in Scotland with a cathedral and a royal mint. However, being close to the English frontier it was constantly subject to surprise attack and at the end of the reign of James II, it was completely dismantled by the Scots.

From *Idyllis of the King* – Gustav Doré

From *Idyllis of the King* –
Gustav Doré

Merlin – The Druid Versus the Saint

The druids were the Celtic intelligentsia. They were men and women of the highest-ranking nobility. The Celts had always been an essentially rural people, depending mainly on subsistence agriculture. Large settlements were alien to their way of life. So the Druids were itinerant, moving from one settlement to another but belonging to none. The Romans had done their best to eradicate them wherever they could.

The dispersed cellular organisation of the Celts with its itinerant aristocracy was the complete opposite to Roman system of centralised authority.

For exactly the same reason, the early Christians had been equally persecuted because they too operated as a network of cells. But when the Emperor Constantine became converted in 380, everything changed. He established Christianity as the Empire's official religion but restructured it to mirror the imperial political system.

A Caesar and his Consuls were matched with a Pope and Cardinals. Spiritual government became parallel to and supportive of the secular imperial regime. Church organisation was now equally hierarchical and totalitarian, with control centred on Rome. Opposition was heresy. The Church's power was based on acquiring wealth and its appeal to the ruling elite. It reinforced their position and interests with the doctrine of the divine right of kings. It was a brilliant way of controlling by influence what Rome could no longer hold by the sword.

Druids were the keepers of knowledge in a society where oral memory was more important than the written word. As healers, diviners and shaman priests they were the go-betweens with the Other World. As tribal historians, bards and poets and as the guardians of lore and knowledge, they passed on the skills of artistry and craftsmanship. Technical training, and the acquirement of magic that went with it, was a lengthy process. Their role was part practical and part spiritual. Learning was the key to power. Oratory and eloquence were considered more powerful than physical strength – and were skills which were honed with age.

In time, the druids' religious duties was taken over by Christian priests but the Druids continued in their other disciplines as 'men of learning' with specialist roles as judges, lawyers, historians, teachers, philosophers, astronomers, prophets, healers, councillors, political advisors, poets, composers and musicians.

In the Arthur legend, Merlin (*Myrddin*) plays an important role, though, in reality, the two almost certainly never met. Merlin was two generations later than Arthur. It is believed that he was a great grandson of Old King Coel through the family who ruled the Rhegged. It was quite common for royal younger sons to become druids and Merlin was at the court of the Ceido, chief of Caer Guendoleu, a generational sub-chiefdom with its capital at Carlisle.

When Ceidio's eldest son, Gwain, came of age, he was sent on a courtesy visit to introduce himself at the Gododdin court. During his stay, he either seduced or raped one of Lot's Christian daughters. She was called Thenau. She was a pious girl who studied Latin, languages and the lore of herbs and flowers with an Irish nun. Was she perhaps part of the religious community founded by St Monenna? In any event, she became pregnant.

The cliff on Dunpender (Traprain) Law

Low tide on the foreshore at Culross

Lot was incensed. Social order was based on the ties of kinship and marriage. As we have seen with Guinevere, unauthorised relationships threatened social stability and were considered to be as destructive as murder. Fornication was treason and Lot had no choice. He condemned Thenau to be hurled off the cliff in a chariot from the summit of the old Gododdin capital on Dunpender (Traprain Law). Amazingly, she landed on soft ground and survived.

Her mother (Arthur's sister) and the other Christians believed it was a miracle but Lot called it witchcraft and now condemned her to death by drowning.

St Serf, Thenau and Mungo

She was strapped into a leather coracle and towed out into the Firth of Forth, where she was cast loose just off the Isle of May. She somehow managed to reach the Maidenhair Rock where, for several hours, she clung to the seaweed – long enough for the tide to turn. Praying to God for help, she was carried slowly up the Forth and beached on the shore not far from St Serf's mission at Culross.

Alone on the foreshore, she gave birth to a son. A passer-by discovered them and carried them to St Serf at the monastery.

Culross Abbey

Both survived and St Serf named the boy Mungo, 'beloved one'.

Brought up by the monks, the boy eventually took holy orders and, at the age of 25, set off as a missionary. In Alt Clut, he founded many churches, not least Glasgow Cathedral and was also known as Kentigern and he was later canonised.

Mungo became so popular and influential in Alt Clut that the chief began to see him as a political challenge, so he banished him to Wales. But his successor Rydderich Hael of Lanark, an ardent Christian committed to spreading the Word to every corner of his territory, immediately recalled Mungo (by now in his late 40s).

There was still a strong Christian nucleus around Whithorn but in much of Galloway, in what is now Dumfriesshire, and in Caer Guendalou round Carlisle, the Druids retained their former status.

Myrddin (Merlin) was chief druid in Carlisle. Gwain had succeeded his father but he seems to have been no great diplomat. In 573, his brother, the High Chief of Ebrauc (York), his cousin, the High Chief of Gwynned, and Rydderich Hael, High Chief of Alt Clut, all joined forces to depose him.

The campaign is said to have lasted six weeks. Gwain's final encampment was at Carwinley (on the southern bank of the Esk). He met his attackers at Arthuret (*Adderyd*) and

The river Esk

The site of the battle on the banks of the Esk

Church commemorating the Christian victory at Adderyd

was killed in the battle. According to custom, his death should have marked the end of the fighting. But on this occasion, it continued. Gwain's pagan army was massacred. Three hundred men were killed and buried nearby.

Myrddin's (Merlin's) sister, Gwenddydd, was married to Rhydderich Hael and, at some stage, probably for her marriage, Merlin had visited Dumbarton, where his pagan presence must have been like a red rag to a bull for the fanatical Rhydderich Hael. In the battle, Merlin is said to have killed her son (his nephew) who was fighting with Rhydderich Hael on the Christian side. She never spoke to him again. The *Black Book of Carmarthen* records that the death of his chief, the slaughter of his tribe and killing his own nephew drove Merlin out of his mind. Identified by the gold torque of his status, perhaps he was allowed to leave the field. Or maybe he just escaped. In any event, he disappeared into the forest of Caledon where it is said that 140 other men of rank also suffered battle madness and perished.

Rydderich Hael built a chapel to commemorate the victory and to the glory of his Christian God. On the site today, there stands a beautiful medieval church.

Merlin did not perish. He travelled north and holed up in a cleugh in the hills, just below the ridge of Hart Fell in what is now Dumfriesshire. Two miles off the old Roman road north from Carlisle and 1,000 feet higher up,

Right:
Hart Fell

Below Left:
Merlin's view of the valley below

Below Right:
The Cleugh

he lived off what the forest could provide and the charity of visitors. Nowadays, the hills are bare but in Merlin's time they would have been densely forested. But not so in the cleugh where Merlin made his hideaway. It is gloomy, hidden from view and a place of utter desolation – a gully of black rocks and scree where nothing grows except for the occasional patch of grass and heather beside the burn – a dead end which even the most casual passer by would hesitate to enter. To reach it is a steep climb up the side of a burn littered with the carcasses of dead sheep caught in winter blizzards. Here Merlin built a rock shelter and lived at the mercy of the elements 'snow to my knees, ice in my beard… I slept alone in the Woods of Celyddon, shield on my shoulder, sword on my thigh'.

A Rock Shelter

There is a chalybeate spring (Hartfell Spa) which was discovered in 1748. It is covered in a small, stone vaulted cellar, roofed with grass and heather and, as late as 1831, it was famous for curing ulcers. Rich in iron and calcium, the water would also be good for rheumatism and doubtless Merlin would have been aware of its health giving properties.

Just above the spring is a rock which once had a massive overhang but which has now fallen. This could have been the site of Merlin's rock shelter. The *Black Book of Carmarthen* talks of a 'cave' but, although there are a number of overhangs where the floor could be deepened, there are no real caves of any size or depth in the cleugh. Right at the top of the gully there is a hidden, very small cave, only reached by scaling the rockface. This might have provided a hiding place in an emergency but could not have served as a regular dwelling. Maybe Merlin vanished here on the approach of unwelcome visitors and so gave rise to the legend that he could transform himself into a hart.

From *Idyllis of the King* –
Gustav Doré

Merlin lived in constant fear of Rhydderich Hael and his Christian cohorts, who now travelled, preaching and converting in the lands below, but keenly aware of Merlin lurking somewhere in his forest hideout. Merlin was equally aware of Mungo; 'I am hated by Rydderich's strongest scion'. It was reciprocal, each saw the other as a champion of an evil falsehood.

For ten years and 40 days, Merlin remained in hiding, nursing his grief, perched up in his desolate moonscape and surrounded lower down by a few scattered settlements where the Selgovae farmers were among the last to remain pagan.

In 583, Merlin finally abandoned his cave and came out of hiding. He realised he was nearing he end of his life and it was time for a final confrontation. He made his way north to what is now the village of Drumelzier on the upper reaches of the Tweed. The name comes from Dun Meldred (Meldred's

Stobo Kirk

Fort) and above the village are the ruins of Tinnis Castle (*Dinas* means stronghold). Meldred was still pagan, as were his kin, but Mungo had founded a church on a druid site, two miles downstream at Stobo – a site still in use today.

Here, the Christian Holy Man confronted the powerful Druid. They must have harangued each other loudly – two old men in a stand off argument of prayer and magic. Something happened. Had the slaughter at Adderyd (Arthuret), which had destroyed Merlin's world and driven him into hiding as a hermit in the forest wilderness, perhaps made him doubt the strength of the old Gods? Did Christianity appear to offer greater supernatural powers? Merlin was an old man and could see death round the corner. Indeed, he had predicted his own 'triple death'. Perhaps he wanted to make his final peace with God.

He was converted. He took communion from St Mungo at a place halfway between Stobo and Drumelzier where an altar of pagan sacrifice is still known as 'the altar stane'. Shortly afterwards, he was confronted by his pagan followers who accused him of betraying his faith and the old gods.

On the banks of the Tweed, he was stoned and beaten before falling backwards into the river to be impaled on to a fisherman's stake. He slipped below the water and was simultaneously drowned. Thus he fulfilled his prophesy of a 'triple death'.

St Mungo lived on until 601 when he died in his mid-80s. Apart from the fact that both Merlin and

Top:
The Alter Stane

Above:
Merlin receives communion across the Powsail Burn

Left:
Merlin's grave marked by the fenced off thorn bush on the right

Arthur suffered a final defeat, there was no connection between them. Half a century separated the two events and it was the medieval storytellers who brought the two characters together to spin a better yarn.

There was an old prophesy: 'When Tweed and Powsail meet at Merlin's grave, Scotland and England shall one monarch have.'

The very day that James VI of Scots also became the First of England, the River Tweed burst its banks at the mouth of the Powsail Burn at Merlin's Grave, – something it never did before or since.

Merlindale in the Upper Tweed by Drumelzier

The Last of 'The Men of the North'

In 547, the Angles captured Dun Guyardi, the capital of Bryneich, gradually expanding inland and up the coast. Rydderich Heal had earned a reputation as a generous High Chief, a great warrior and a devout Christian. Around 590, he formed a coalition with the Scots of Dalriada, the Scots of Antrim in Northern Ireland and the Gododdin and together they embarked on a crusade which drove the Angles back to their last strongholds of Dun Guyardi (Bamburgh) and Holy Island. Gawain (the religious absentee High Chief of the Gododdin) had been succeeded by his son Morcant who, through marriage, had also become Chief of Bryneich. The Bryneich and the Gododdin had always been the same people. Now Rydderich offered Bryneich to the Irish Scots. Morcant considered this nothing short of betrayal and promptly assassinated Rydderich. The British coalition dissolved overnight. The Angles escaped annihilation and the whole course of British history was changed.

The Venerable Bede wrote:

> the kings, priests, private men, and the nobility still remembering the late calamities and slaughters, in some measure kept within bounds; but when these died, and another generation succeeded, which knew nothing of those times, and was only acquainted with the present peaceable state of things, all the bonds of justice and sincerity were so entirely broken, that there was not only no trace of them remaining, but few persons seemed to be aware that such virtues had ever existed.

Dun Guyardi
(Bamburgh)

Holy Island

Seventeen years later in the closing years of the 7th century, a cavalry force of 363 Gododdin set out from Dun Eidyn to confront an attacking force of Angles. They were reinforced by contingents from North Wales, Rhegged and Alt Clut.

300 torques, war like, well trained
300 haughty, in harmony, armed,
300 fierce steeds bore them to battle
3 hounds, 300; tragic, no return.

They met at Catterick and, although the Gododdin were reputed to have slain seven times their own number, they were overwhelmed. They fought to the death and perished with only three survivors. One of them, Aneirin, wrote the elegiac poem *Y Gododdin* – a tribute to his comrades who fell in battle. The poem is preserved in a mid-13th century copy *The Book of Aneirin*. It records a defeat which exalts the heroism of warriors who have no fear of death and, in dying, win fame and honour.

He thrust beyond 300, most bold, he cut down the centre and far wing
He proved worthy, leading noble men; he gave from his herds steeds for winter
He brought black crows to a fort's walls, though he was no Arthur
He made his strength a refuge, the front line's bulwark, Gwawrddar.

It is clear from the poem that the cavalry were Gododdin cavalry. There is no mention of the Manau. By this time it had been absorbed into Alt Clut as Britain splintered into an ever-increasing number of autonomous petty chiefdoms. It finally fell to the Angles in 638 and, within two years, Gododdin had ceased to exist.

BRITAIN circa
630 AD

NORTHERN
PICTAVIA

SOUTHERN
PICTAVIA

SCOTS

Dun Eidyn

Alt Clut

Gododdin

YR HEN OGLEDD

Selcovia

Rhegged

ANGLES

CYMRU

SAXONS

DUMNONIA

Arno Vilanove

Conclusion

The starting point of this investigation has been the writings of Gildas in the 6th century and Nennius in the 8th. Placing the events they described within the broader perspective of what we also know of the history, politics, economics and personalities of the period has provided the basis of a conjectural hypothesis. It can only be based on the notion, so abhorrent to academics, that there is no smoke without fire. There are no hard and proven facts – only possibilities. But within the range of conjecture, there are varying degrees of probability.

Did Arthur really exist? It seems highly probable.

Who was Arthur? He was certainly of a noble family and most probably was brought up amongst the Men of the North. What better training ground for a young warrior than to be attached to the crack cavalry of the Manau?

Was his real name Arthur? Debatable but certainly it was his *nom de guerre*.

Who were the enemy? In the south, Angles and Saxons were gaining footholds on the coast but, in the north, the threat to the Britons was and always had been the Picts.

Manau was created as a military zone and, in the last days of the Romans, manned entirely by Britons but who reported to the Roman military HQ in York. By Arthur's time, it seems to have still been autonomous mainly under Alt Clut influence, who had replaced the Gododdin as the most powerful and wealthiest of the North British tribes. When Arthur died, Manau was inherited by a younger brother of the High Chief of Alt Clut to whom Arthur was probably related. It was expanded to take in part of Gododdin and renamed the chiefdom of Dun Eidyn (with another younger brother holding the title of Chieftain of Manau).

It seems highly probable that Arthur's first six battles were in response to a Pictish victory in the Lennox district, and linked to the fall of the House of Caw.

It would have been a logical strategy to consolidate the success of these earlier battles by knocking out the forward bases of the Southern Picts. Archaeological evidence indicates that this occurred but whether it was actually in Arthur's time we do not yet know.

Arthur was a Christian and his campaigns were also crusades, reinforcing the strength of the new faith.

If the hypothesis is correct, the result was that Arthur diffused the threat of the Southern Picts. If not, it is hard to explain why for the next 30 years there was peace.

There is no evidence of much social interchange between the untamed and backward Selgovae and the other northern Briton tribes. Indeed, Gododdin and Alt Clut had been paid for centuries to help keep them bottled up and isolated in the remote forest of the Southern Uplands, so there was no love lost between them and inter-relations appear to have been minimal. If not directly involved, Arthur certainly helped to create the conditions for their final integration into the Alt Clut, thus securing the internal cohesion of the lands north of the Wall.

In the west, there was an alliance with the Scots. Immediately before and during Arthur's time, there was massive immigration from Ireland and peace on the well-defended Alt Clut front allowed the Scots to concentrate on expansion in the sparsely populated Pictish lands to the north.

Did Arthur go south and take command of the Great Army? It is recorded that the Great Army was reinforced by the Gododdin cavalry but that is all we know. There is no mention of Arthur.

At the Battle of Badon, Nennius states that the confederate army was under the command of Arthur. The battle is recorded in the history of both sides, Saxon and Briton, and there was no attempt at the further expansion of Wessex westwards for at least a generation.

As a name, Camelot does not appear until the legends of the Middle Ages, so its existence is debatable. But the port of Camelon did exist and was still an important centre of trade in Arthur's time.

The establishment of St Monenna's various religious houses seems to mirror quite closely the movements of Arthur's campaigns.

Eccles (St Ninians) was well established as a Christian mission and is almost certainly where Arthur would have been buried. In *The Lives of the Saints*, St Ninian and St Monenna are quite probably composites of more than one person. But if, as may be the case with Arthur as well, they did not exist, someone like them did.

And finally, there is Merlin – the last of the Druids. He really did exist but two generations later than Arthur and there was no connection between the two.

Perhaps, one day, we will have proven answers but, for now, all we can do is try to arrive at informed probability. The discovery of the truth lies in the hands of archaeologists. Only they can finally clear the obscurity of the Dark Ages. Until then, the true story of Arthur remains a mystery with an open ending.

From *Idyllis of the King* – Gustav Doré

The Development of The Legend

In the 12th century, the stories of Arthur moved from semi-factual Celtic record to international fiction. Geoffrey de Monmouth was the first to popularise Arthur with his *Historia Regum Britanniae* in 1137. He took a Celtic champion and turned him into a Norman hero.

De Monmouth was born, on the Welsh border, of an aristocratic family originating in Brittany. He was a monk with ambition and, although he probably had a smattering of Welsh and Breton, his first language was Norman. Together with another author, Gerald of Wales, it was they who really popularised the Arthurian legend in England, taking historical events but setting them in Cornwall and Somerset. Gerald of Wales claimed to have been an eyewitness to the exhumation of Arthur's remains at Glastonbury Abbey.

This relocation was undoubtedly deliberate. Henry I was the first of his line and concerned to secure the Plantagenet succession. He would not have appreciated a romance which might have appealed to Welsh nationalism. The Normans had only been in England for 70 years but their empire also extended into Wales and Ireland and covered much of France. So it was only politique that Arthur now also assumed a continental dimension.

Apart from the Arthurian traditions in Wales and South West England, there is also a strong Arthurian tradition in Brittany where he is associated with the Foret de Brocéliande. As we have seen in the case of Merlin, Geoffrey de Monmouth was not averse to combining unconnected elements to make a better and more international story.

The Normans were masters of integration and assimilation. They ruled Celts, Angles, Saxons and Frenchmen. Geoffrey de Monmouth created an Arthur with whom all the peoples could identify. In the *Historia*, he conquers the Picts and the Irish, annexes Iceland, Norway and Denmark as well as Gaul and is on the point of crossing the Alps to sort out the Roman Emperor when he is

Henry II Norman
Kingdom

recalled to deal with the treacherous Mordred (Medraut). Is there a historical basis for this European dimension?

A sixth century historian, Jordane, recorded the exploits of another British war chief called Riothamus. The name means 'Chief of Chiefs'. The distinction between South West England and Brittany may not have had much meaning at that time. They were the same people, spoke the same language and perhaps, like the Scots in Northern Ireland and Scotland, for a time may have shared a common High Chief. In the face of Saxon invasion, there had been massive imigration from Britain.

Hard pressed by the Visigoth invasions, Rome asked Riothamus to come with reinforcements to help save Gaul. He crossed the Channel with an army reputedly of 12,000 men. The year was 468. But before he could meet up with the Roman army, he was engaged by the Visigoths in the Upper Loire valley. In the ensuing battle, he lost the greater part of his men and fled with his remaining forces to Bergundy. His last known position was near the Bergundian town of Avallon. Is this perhaps where 'Avalon' is borrowed from? Riothamus was already an established French hero and, in assuming his mantle, Arthur became immediately familiar.

Avallon is a hilltop town surrounded by the dense Morvan Forest. It is renowned for the apples, cherries and vines that grow on its terraced slopes. In Arthur's time, the surrounding area was liable to flooding and so like Glastonbury, Avallon could from time to time become a virtual island. It was also a centre of healing and a Roman spa. A nearby lake, Les Fontaines Salées, contains helium which bubbles to the surface, giving the place a quite magical quality. The waters also contain a high density of salt as well as sodium, chlorine, sulphur, chalk, magnesium and iron – a chemical cocktail extremely effective in the treatment of burns and wounds. Archaeological excavations have revealed a huge quantity of votive offerings which over the centuries had been thrown into the water.

In the legend, Geoffrey de Monmouth says that Excalibur was made in Avalon and on his death thrown into the lake. Just outside the town the Roman Camp Coro was, for a long time, a base for a cavalry unit recruited from a tribe of Near Eastern nomadic horsemen. Here Celtic and Near Eastern metallurgical skills had combined to create a renowned centre of excellence for the forging of weaponry and chain mail. Was Riothamus' sword thrown into the waters of Les Fointaines Salées? Was it perhaps also subsequently recovered? Six centuries later Richard the Lionheart and Phillip II of France set off from the Basilica of Vézelay in 1190 at the start of the 3rd Crusade. Vézelay is just ten miles from Avallon. A crusader wrote that here Richard was presented with Arthur's Excalibur to take with him to the Holy Land. This was a year before the supposed 'discovery' of Arthur's tomb at Glastonbury.

Avallon today and as it was

A hundred years before Riothamus there was also Maximus who had served under Theodosius in Africa, on the Danube and during the Great Conspiracy in Britain where, afterwards, he remained. When Theodosius became Emperor of the Eastern Empire, Maximus declared himself Emperor of the Western Empire and, with most of the military manpower in Britain, crossed the Channel and invaded Europe. He defeated the Western Emperor Gratian and ruled Britain, Gaul and Spain for four years before he, in his turn, was defeated and killed. Meantime he gave Brittany (Armorica), as a reward, to his second in command, Conan, where modern British historians generally give some credence to the idea of a mass British troop settlement.

By combining all these disparate elements, Geoffrey de Monmouth created a medieval best-seller, drawing on historical events and characters but combining them into composites to make a politically correct story. It was an artistic license which cut across ethnic identities – a story with which all the disparate parts of Henry II's empire could identify. It was good Plantagenet political propaganda and Geoffrey was duly rewarded with a bishopric.

The *Historia* was the mainspring of the stories which followed during the Middle Ages. It tells of the miraculous circumstances of Arthur's birth. It also introduces Excalibur, the sword forged in Avalon, his coronation at the age of 15 and his marriage to Guinevere.

From *Idyllis of the King* – Gustav Doré

Arthur is the conquering hero, brave, sometimes dictatorial, a defender of the faith, living in luxury and surrounded by the greatest knights. He is a king (in old Welsh *Arth Ru* means High Chief or King – did Monmouth confuse *Arth Ru* with Arthur?). He battles a giant (King Caw was said to be a giant of a man). He lead successful campaigns in Ireland and Gaul. He takes on the might of the Roman army and marches on Rome but in his absence is betrayed by Mordred who has seized power at home. Arthur returns to confront him in the final battle of Camlann where Mordred is killed and Arthur is mortally wounded and taken to Avalon. Merlin is presented as a half mad prophet who lives in the dark forests of Northumberland and stirs up trouble with his powers of magic and enchantment.

De Monmouth's *Historia*, was written in Latin. It was quickly followed by a Norman French adaptation in Wace's *Le Roman de Brut* in 1155 and a version in English in 1190 by a priest called Layamin. Wace introduced the Round Table and the tradition that a feast was always preceded with an account of an adventure by one of the knights. Arthur embodies all the virtues of chivalry. A perfect ruler of a model court, an immortal whose ultimate return is predicted by Merlin. Arthur is not dead but just sleeping at Avalon, awaiting the day when he will return to rule over a united Britain.

In the period 1170–90, the troubadours were at their height and in the stories of Chrétien de Troyes, Arthur begins to take second place to the exploits of the Knights of the Round Table. Sir Gawain and Sir Lancelot are the heroes of amazing adventures and, in *Perceval the Story of the Grail,* are introduced to the subtleties of courtly love and the quest for the Holy Grail. There was always a market for sex interest.

The knights errant are adventurers who set out alone on a quest to seek fame, love and fortune. Usually someone

From *Idyllis of the King* – Gustav Doré

comes to court looking for help and a knight sets off to the rescue. They battle with dragons and monsters. They encounter dwarfs and giants. They overcome brigands who rape, pillage and murder. They experience the seductive powers of beautiful sorceresses and overcome the fiends of the Devil. Their mission complete, they return to recount their adventures at court where Arthur's scribes record them for posterity.

The damsels in distress are usually unattainable and of higher rank than the knight. Undaunted, he sets out to win her love by defeating her enemies, rescuing her from the hands of villains who have abducted her or by finding some important object on which she has set her heart. He is the soul of discretion, totally devoted and altruistic. The adultery of Tristan and Isolde or Lancelot and Guinevere are moral tales, highlighting the potential danger of conflicting loyalties caused on the one hand by infidelity in marriage through extramarital affairs and on the other hand, by duty between vassal and lord.

Robert de Boron (1190–1210) further developed the Holy Grail theme and established it as the cup which held the blood of Christ which was brought to Britain by Joseph of Arimathea. Christianity now adopted the old Celtic legends for its own liturgical propaganda and Merlin becomes the son of the devil, opposed to the coming of Christianity. God gives him the gift of being able to see the future and to be an instrument of goodness. Merlin arranges the birth and the ultimate recognition of Arthur as king. But his love for the Lady of the Lake and his weakness of the flesh proves to be his undoing.

In the 12th and 13th centuries, the stories of the Knights of the Round Table were written to entertain the leading aristocracy. They represented an ideal for feudal society. Writers in Holland, Norway, Portugal, Spain, Italy and Germany all contributed to the legends. There was even a Hebrew version. All levels of society began to give their children Arthurian names. It was a fashion which lasted until the end of the 15th century.

Sir Gawain and the Green Knight appeared in the late 1300s (author unknown) and Thomas Malory's *Morte d'Arthur* was published and printed by Caxton in 1485. He was perhaps the most influential of the medieval writers. Arthur returns to centre stage – now an English hero capable of creating a continental empire. The political effect can be measured by the fact that Henry VII even named his eldest son Arthur. He was born a year after publication but died in 1502, the same year as his father, and, by papal decree, his 17-year-old wife, Catherine of Aragon, was remarried to Arthur's 12-year-old younger brother Henry VIII.

The advent of printing gave the stories a new life. In Paris, the printer Antoine Vérard also played a major role in publishing the stories and even produced luxury illustrated editions on vellum.

In 1596, Edmund Spenser published *The Faerie Queene* – an incomplete epic poem. It was planned as 24 books – 12 exemplifying the virtues of 12 knights and another 12 centred on Arthur himself. It presented the exciting possibility of an English Protestant empire ruled over by a virgin queen – herself an improved and enlightened female version of King Arthur.

By the end of the 18th century, the stories of Arthur and The Knights of the Round Table had virtually disappeared from library shelves but with the romantic revival in the early 19th century, they made a come-back. Malory's *Morte d'Arthur* was reprinted and Tennyson wrote his first Arthurian poem *The Lady of Shalot* in 1833. Gustav Doré illustrated *The Idylls of a King* which, as poet laureate, Tennyson dedicated to Prince Albert. It reflected the ideals and morality of the mid-Victorian period.

Arthur represents an 'ideal of manhood'. The finding of spiritual fulfilment in the purest form of romantic love was very much in line with Victorian ideals and Guinevere fails by not living up to the purity expected of her. By royal command, the Queen's Robing Rooms in the new palace of Westminster were decorated with frescoes of the Arthurian legends which became a popular subject of the Pre-Raphaelites. In Germany, Wagner reworked the stories as operatic librettos.

Later writers such as Apollinaire, Jean Cocteau, Mark Twain, John Steinbeck, Tolkein and Tolstoy also found inspiration in the legends. During the Second World War, with Britain facing imminent invasion by the Germans, T.H. White wrote the first of the four books of *The Once and Future King* and these in turn inspired films musicals and TV series. Walt Disney introduced Arthur to Hollywood. Today, the Internet teems with Arthur computer games and a plethora of Arthuriana sites.

Arthur has it all – sex and violence, loyalty and betrayal, love and infidelity, revenge, rape, adultery, incest, the holy grail, monsters, giants, the supernatural – every element a scriptwriter ever dreamed of and, of course, a brilliant cast of goodies, baddies, wizards and powerful women – the ideal palette of a Hollywood blockbuster.

From *Idyllis of the King* –
Gustav Doré

In each century, the Arthurian legend has been reworked to reflect the colours of the times. Over the 1,500 years since his death, Arthur has metamorphosed from a shadowy military hero in Celtic Britain into an immortal super hero, encapsulating the romanticism and ideals of successive centuries, to rule a world of fantasy and escapism.

Timeline

AD

70	Roman Conquest of Northern England.
79–83	Agricola invades Scotland and makes a treaty with the Votadini (Gododdin) and Alt Clut (Damnoni).
123	Hadrian builds a wall from the Tyne to the Solway.
138	Antonine occupies Southern Scotland and builds a Wall from the Forth to the Clyde.
152	Antonine Wall abandoned.
208–210	Severus campaigns in Scotland and advances to the Moray Firth before retreating and rebuilding Hadrian's Wall.
211–410	Gododdin cavalry undertake defence north of Hadrian's Wall against the Picts.
347	Bones of St Andrew brought to Scotland.
367	Picts, Scots and Saxons overrun the North of England.
370	**Manau cavalry established** as part of Valentia protectorate with other cavalry forces in Alt Clut, Gododdin and Galwyddel.
384	Chester abandoned.
387	Roman garrisons withdrawn from the Pennines. Magnus Maximus crosses with his army from Britain to Armorica (Britanny).
397	St Ninian brings Christianity to Whithorn on the Solway.
407	**The legions abandon Britain** and Coel Hen, last military governor of Britain north of the Mersey/Humber based in York declares himself High Chief of N. Britain. South of the Mersey/Humber line Vortigern is High Chief of Britain.
420?	Manau cavalry, retakes West Wales from Scots settlers and founds the Welsh royal dynasty.
429	Picts and Scots raiders expelled from Southern Britain by Jutes, Angles and Saxons.

432	Death of St Ninian and birth of St Monenna in Ireland.
436	**Last Roman mercenary troops recalled.**
437	Kent abandoned to the Jutes.
449	Vortigern invites Saxon mercenaries to defend his coasts from Pictish raiders.
450	Missionaries from Whithorn start conversion of Southern Picts.
455	Picts attack Britain in support of the Saxon rebellion.
457	Death of Vortigern. Accession of Ambrosius Aurelianus who defeats the Saxons.
460	St Patrick excommunicates Ceretic of Alt Clut for profiting from slavery.
460	Fergus arrives in Dalriada, allies with the Picts. Defeat and death of Coel Hen in Ayrshire and his chiefdom is subdivided E/W of the Pennines into Ebrauc and Rhegged.
460	Lot appointed High Chief of Gododdin. Ceretic of Alt Clut Bryneich made into a separate high chiefdom.
461	South East Britain finally lost to Saxons.
468	Rothiamus defeated and retreats to Avallon.
470–475?	**Birth of Arthur.**
476	Fall of Rome.
477	Foundation of Kingdom of Sussex.
480	South of a line from the Humber to the Solent occupied by Jutes, Angles and Saxons.
495–516?	**Likely period of Arthur's campaigns – 12 battles.**
499	Foundation of Kingdom of Wessex.
500	Fresh wave of Scots immigration from Ireland to Dalriada
501	Deposition of Caw of Alt Clut. Succeeded by Dumnagual. Hen Saxons take Portsmouth.
503	Death of Fergus King of Scots.
507	Abdication of Dumnaguel Hen.
508	Battle of Bassas. Death of the sons of Caw. Accession of Clinoch Saxons land at Southampton Water.

510?	Death of King Lot. Gawain succeeds.
516	Battle of Badon.
518?	**Death of St Monenna.**
530	Saxons take Isle of Wight.
535–540	Volcanic ash/meteor causes climate change. Plague.
537?	**Battle of Camlann and death of Arthur.**
538	Comgall, King of Scots killed by Picts.
547	Angles take Bamburgh.
552	Saxons take Old Sarum (Dorchester).
550s	Major migrations from Britain to Armorica (Brittany).
558	Gabran, King of Scots killed by Picts.
563	St Columba founds Iona Abbey.
570	Death of Gildas.
573?	**Battle of Arthuret. Merlin flees to the forest.**
583	**Merlin confronts St Mungo. Triple death of Merlin.**
583–590	Men of the North led by Rydderich Heal defeat the Angles but he is murdered before the final decisive battle and victory is dissipated.
601	Death of St Mungo.
603	Angle victory at Degsestan (Liddesdale) over combined armies of Bernicia and Dalriada.
640	Gododdin falls to the Angles.
858	Union of Picts and Scots.
870	Alt Clut falls to the Vikings.
	End of Briton culture in Yr Hen Ogledd (Men of the North).
12th C	Old Welsh (Brythonic) language dies out in Southern Scotland.

From a stone in
Govan Old Parish Kirk

APPENDIX I

The Roman Occupation

The Romans invaded Britain in 43AD and quickly occupied and colonised the fertile South. What is now the North of England was the territory of the Brigantes, a hotbed of resistance with whom all efforts to negotiate a lasting peace failed. So finally the Roman strategists decided that security depended on the subjugation of the whole of Britain. In around 70AD they marched north, defeated the Brigantes, established a legionary HQ at York and then swung westward to conquer Wales. The Brigantes retreated into the heavily forested uplands of the Pennines.

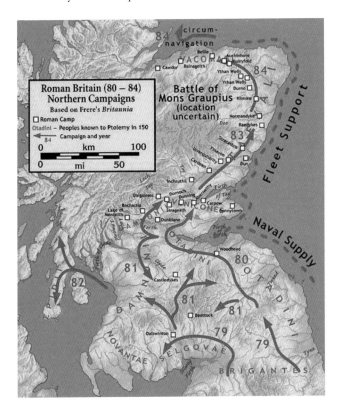

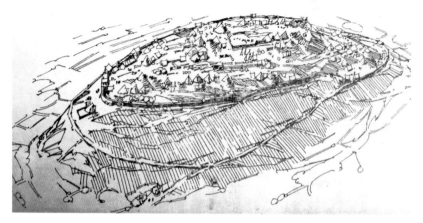

Throughout the Empire, the Romans had always protected their frontiers by treaties with semi-autonomous client kingdoms. By serving as buffer states, these benefited from regular handouts of 'overseas aid' and the commercial opportunities of trade with Rome. This was Agricola's tactic with the Votadini (Gododdin) who occupied the east coast, north of the Roman garrison at York and right up to the Firth of Forth. They were guaranteed autonomy in return for a laissez-passer for the Roman army. This was the beginning of a 'special relationship' which was to endure for the next 300 years.

On the western boundary of the Votadini (Gododdin), in what is now the Scottish Southern Uplands, were the Selgovae – 'the hunters'. They occupied an area of dense Caledonian forest which in the south joined up with the Pennines and the Brigantes. The Votadini (Gododdin) and the Selgovae territory is dotted with hillforts and defended settlements. The capital of the Votadini (Gododdin) was on Traprain Law in East Lothian. An earthen rampart enclosed 40 acres on top of a 500ft high hill.

In Dumfriesshire in the west, the Selgovae were bordered by the Novantae (Galwyddel) – a tribe occupying Galloway and the Isle of Man. The Novantae lived in fortified, isolated farmsteads. Some are crannogs – artificial platforms built on piles in lochs and approachable only by boat or narrow

causeways. Other farms were centred on brochs – massive circular towers up to 40 feet high, or else were oval or circular enclosures surrounded by a strong stone wall.

The area which is today's Ayrshire and Strathclyde and which reached slightly north of the Clyde was occupied by the Damnoni – the miners (Alt Clut) with whom Agricola made a similar treaty so that Clyde and the Forth could then be supplied by sea by the Roman navy.

The dense forests of the Southern Uplands were difficult terrain for the Romans – impossible for tight formations

Forest – ideal cover for Guerrilla warfare

and perfect cover for guerrilla tactics and ambush by the highly mobile Celts. So Agricola's strategy was to march north in a pincer movement, with the 20th legion in the west and the 9th on the east who would join up in the Forth Clyde valley, circumventing the Selgovae in the Central Southern Uplands. The Selgovae and their allies the Novantae (Galwyddel) of Galloway resisted. The outcome was decisive. They were decimated and the Selgovae withdrew into the forest and the hills in the centre. A line of forts isolated them from the Novantae in the west and protected the road which the Romans built along the line of the present M74 linking Carlisle with the Clyde. Another road in the east, Dere Street, was built along the line of the present A68 and followed the Selgovae-Votadini (Gododdin) border. Each enabled the rapid movement of troops.

Two years later, in 81AD the Novantae (Galwyddel) in Galloway and their northern neighbours the Damnoni (Alt Clut) in Strathclyde rose against the Romans and were put down. The Votadini (Gododdin) remained loyal. Agricola consolidated his position in the Forth Clyde valley with a turf wall which later became the base of the Antonine Wall. Then, in 82AD, he advanced north to the Tay, building a line of forts and signal stations at the foot of the Highland glens to bottle up the Picts.

Agricola had an army, the like of which the Picts had never seen before. It was a blitzkrieg, with the Roman army advancing from the south and the Roman navy attacking the Picts' previously safe havens on both the west and east coasts. The Picts avoided confrontation in a major battle and settled down to a prolonged guerrilla war of hit and run attacks on soft targets and lines of supply.

In 83AD supported by his navy, Agricola advanced into Aberdeenshire. A surprise night attack by the Picts nearly annihilated the 9th legion who were only saved at the last moment by the Roman cavalry.

The Romans continued their advance and actually reached Inverness. It was a policy of slash and burn, destroying everything in their path and laying waste crops and homesteads.

The Roman navy sailed right round the north coast and Ptolemy mapped Britain as an island for the first time.

Eventually, at 'Mons Graupius', Agricola was confronted in a pitched battle with a confederation of the Pictish tribes under a war chief called Calgacus. It was immediately after the harvest and the Picts were faced with starvation if the Romans destroyed their granaries. The two armies probably met on an ancient trackway across high ground in Kincardineshire beside the Elsick Mounth.

A Roman army of perhaps 20,000 men faced a confederation of around 30,000 Picts. Before the battle, the two opposing generals addressed their troops. The accuracy of the Roman account, written by Tacitus, has to be read as being slanted for a home readership back in Rome. He was writing in Latin but maybe the speech that he attributed to Calgacus, which would have been in Pictish, captures the spirit of the Picts...

> You have mustered to a man and all of you are free. There are no lands behind us and even on the sea we are menaced by the Roman fleet... Battles against Rome have been lost and won before; but hope was never abandoned, since we were always here in reserve. We, the choicest flower of Britain's manhood, were hidden away in her most secret places... We, the most distant dwellers upon earth, the last of the free, have been shielded till today by our very remoteness and by the obscurity in which it has shrouded our name. Now, the farthest bounds of Britain lie open to our enemies; and what men know nothing about they always assume to be a valuable prize. But there are no more nations beyond us; nothing is there but waves and rocks, and the Romans more deadly still than these – for in them is an arrogance which no submission or good behaviour can escape. Pillagers of the world, they have exhausted the land by their indiscriminate plunder, and now they ransack the sea... East and West alike have failed to satisfy them... To robbery, butchery, and rapine, they give the lying name of 'government'. They create a desolation and call it 'peace'.

The Picts held the higher ground and using their greater numbers outflanked the Romans but once again the Roman cavalry came to the rescue. The Picts melted away into the hills.

The following day Tacitus reports

> An awful silence reigned on every hand; the hills were deserted, houses smoking in the distance, and our scouts did not meet a soul.

Both sides had incurred heavy losses and each retired to lick their wounds but the guerrilla tactics and constant harassment by the Picts continued. Uprisings in Germany forced the 9th legion to be withdrawn and Agricola was recalled to Rome. Within three years, the Romans had retreated back to the line, which 30 years later was to become Hadrian's Wall.

The Picts had good relations with the Selgovae in the Central Southern Uplands. Pictish remains suggest that the area once had a Pictish population and that perhaps, for a time, they and the Selgovae lived side-by-side and intermarried. The dense Caledonian Forest, which covered the hills provided excellent cover for Pictish raiding parties who constantly passed through Selgovia to harry the Romans to the south. The war started by Agricola was by no means over.

In 123AD, the Emperor Hadrian built the stone wall, running from Carlisle to Newcastle. It was manned by 10,000 troops whose role was to block any uncontrolled Pictish incursions from the north into the Pennines.

Fifteen years later, the Emperor Antonine built a second wall of wooden palisades on the old Agricola line between the Forth and the Clyde, again to keep out the Pictish raiders. This Antonine Wall held for 20 years, and allowed the treaty with the Votadini on the east coast to develop into a closer and mutually beneficial relationship. A tablet discovered at Vindolanda on Hadrian's Wall reveals that the Romans called them *Brittunculi* – 'the wee Brits'.

Ditch of the Antonine Wall near Twechar

Halfway between the two walls, where Dere Street crossed the river Tweed, the Romans established a major garrison in the shadow of the Eildon Hills – Trimontium. It could be supplied upriver from the sea and was the main supply base for the interwall zone. It was also an important trading post. From the wild interior, the Selgovae brought hides and furs as well as live animals to organised trade fairs. These were held under Roman supervision on the edge of their territory at regular times of the year. There was a demand for live bears for the arenas of Rome. Scotland together with

Panonia in Hungary, was a principle source of supply. The Votadini traded cattle, hides, wool and probably slaves as well, in return for pottery, glass, bronze, iron and silver goods and wine. All roads in the interwall zone were measured from Trimontium – the centre of the system.

It was also an important Roman cavalry training camp, recruiting from the Votadini who were well known as accomplished horsemen. It was manned initially by a regiment of dragoons and a crack light cavalry unit of Voconti, a Celtic tribe in northern Spain and Southern France whose language was very similar to the Old Welsh of the Votadini.

When the Antonine Wall was abandoned in 152AD, the Roman frontier retreated to Hadrian's Wall but Trimontium remained a forward base until 211. After that, it was the northern British tribes who defended their frontiers against the Picts. While remaining semi-autonomous, the Gododdin in particular had learned much through their close association with the Romans in terms of statecraft and military tactics. For the remaining 200 years of Roman occupation south of Hadrian's Wall, the Votadini and the Damnoni acted as a buffer zone. The *pax romana* was a treaty which guaranteed Roman protection. The exact terms for the Votadini have not survived but similar arrangements beyond the Danube suggest a rigorous control of local affairs. Relations with neighbouring tribes were regulated and tribute was exacted.

The tribal gatherings for commerce or other purposes remained strictly limited to fixed times and under Roman supervision. A list of these places survives and indicates that

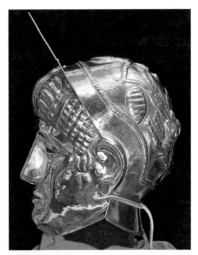

Top:
Ceremonial helmet from Trimontium

Middle:
Antonine Wall at Twechar

Bottom:
Eildon Hills the three mountains of Trimontium with their important Iron Age hillfort

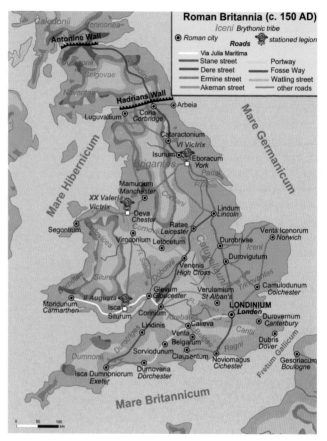

Wikipedia

the Selgovae (the hillbilly hunters of the Southern Uplands) assembled at Locus Maponis (Lochmaben) and possibly also at Locus Segloes [Selgo(v)e(n)s(is)] which may have been near the Roman Fort at Lyne in the Upper Tweed valley (but there is also a school of thought which places Locus Segloes in the Trent area of England). It was perhaps a bit like the trading activities of the Hudson Bay Company with North American Indians. The area was policed by the *exploratores*, mounted scouts who were permanently based at small outposts.

The two Roman walls and the line of forts in the north were built to contain and separate hostile land forces, but throughout the occupation, Pictish raiders still managed to get through. More importantly, they had ships with which they pillaged the coast. By the 4th century, the Romans identified two Pictish confederations – one of tribes to the north of the Grampians and another of tribes to the south. Pictish maritime raiders were joined by Saxon pirates and the Romans were forced to build a chain of coastal watchtowers. The Roman defences were by now seriously undermanned, so they had to rely heavily on a major recruitment of Angle and Saxon mercenaries. On the west coast, Scots from Ireland began to attack and settle from Argyll down to Devon.

This culminated in the Great Conspiracy of 367, which was the start of our story.

Crannog
Loch Tay

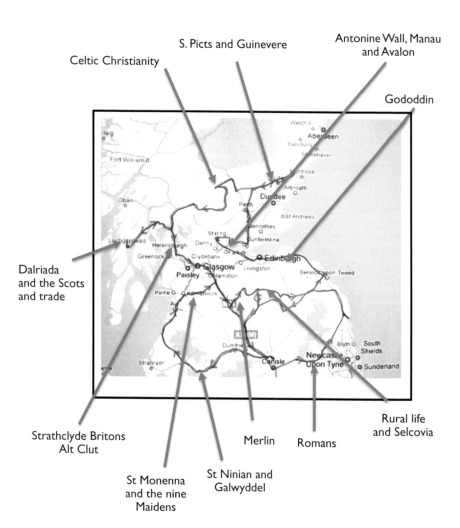

Celtic Christianity

S. Picts and Guinevere

Antonine Wall, Manau and Avalon

Gododdin

Dalriada and the Scots and trade

Strathclyde Britons Alt Clut

St Monenna and the nine Maidens

St Ninian and Galwyddel

Merlin

Romans

Rural life and Selcovia

Gazetteer

The book presents the evidence. You, the reader, can now follow it up on the ground and make your own conclusions. This is an 'Arthur Trail' which takes you on a journey round Southern Scotland on an exploration of forgotten times and forgotten places.

Although there is no law of trespass in Scotland, there are laws of privacy and against disturbing animals, damaging crops, fences or property. So in visiting any of these places please respect any private ownership of sites and their approaches.

Looking For Arthur

An itinerary in the lands of The Old North

The Romans

Carlisle – Castle and Tullie House Museum.
Hadrian's Wall – Vindolanda, The Roman Army Museum, Steel Rigg, Housesteads, Chesters, Arbeia

Bryneich

Alnwick, Alnmouth, Bamburgh, Linsdisfarne, Chillingham, Yeavering Bell, Bremenium (Rochester)

Selgovae/Gododdin

Ruberslaw, Yarrow, Cademuir, Galashiels (Broch and Catrail), Melrose (Roman museum and Trimontium), Merchidun (Roxburgh), Berwick-on-Tweed Traprain Law, Edinburgh Castle, Arthurs Seat, Royal Scottish Museum

Manau

Camelon, Antonine Wall (Watling Lodge and Twechar) Stirling Castle, Cambuskenneth Abbey, Abbey Mount, St Ninians, Clackmannan, Culross

The Picts

Pictavia (Brechin), Meigle Museum, Aberlemno Stone, Eassie, The Crannog Centre (Kenmore), Fortingall (Dun Geal), Inchadney, St Fillans (Dundurn), Clach nam Breatann, Falls of Falloch, Allt Fionn Ghleann, Dubh Eas, Glen Douglas, Arrochar

The Scots

Dunadd, Kilmartin, Crinan, Ben Arthur

Alt Clut

Dumbarton Castle, Govan Museum, Glasgow Cathedral

Merlin

Stobo, Drumelzier, Hart Fell, Arthuret

St Ninian

Whithorn

Aeron

Coyleton, Dundonald, Darvel

The Arthur Trail
The Trail in 12 Days

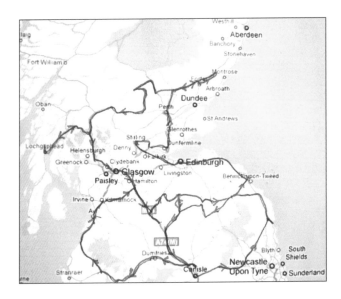

Day 1	**North Northumberland**	Hadrians Wall and the Romans
Day 2	**North Northumberland**	Bryneich
Day 3/4	**Scottish Borders, East Lothian & Edinburgh** Selgovae and Gododdin	
Day 6	**Stirling, Clackmannan & East Fife**	Manau
Day 7	**Angus, Perthshire and the Lennox**	Picts
Day 8	**Argyll**	Scots
Day 9	**Dumbarton & Glasgow**	the Alt Clut
Day 10	**Upper Tweeddale and Dumfriesshire**	Merlin
Day 11	**Galloway**	St Ninian
Day 12	**Ayrshire**	Aeron

ENGLAND York, Bath & Dorset

FRANCE Bergundy (Avallon) and Britanny (Brocéliande)

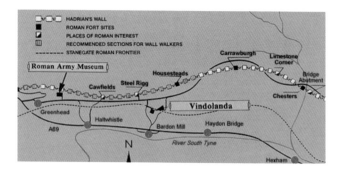

North Northumberland
Hadrian's Wall

See: 'Appendix 1 – The Roman Occupation' and 'The Roman Legacy'

You can easily spend a week on **Hadrians Wall** but here is an itinerary which you can do in a day and will give you the essential flavour.

From Carlisle, travel east on the A69 to Greenhead where you join the B6318 which is the Roman Stanegate – the road which serviced the Wall. Just north of Haltwhistle turn left to the **Roman Army Museum,** which is on the Wall and has an interesting short film in 3D, a birds eye journey giving an impression of the wall as it must have looked in Roman times, as well as an excellent exhibition.

Continue along the Stanegate and at Twice Brewed turn left up to **Steel Rig**, which is one of the best views of the Wall.

Nearby is Milecastle 39 (Castle Nick). There were milecastles all along the wall with a garrison of perhaps 20–30 auxiliary soldiers who also manned two stone towers a third of a Roman mile to the east and to the west. The milecastle's garrison controlled the passage of people, goods and livestock across the frontier, and acted as a customs post to levy taxation on traffic passing through.

Retrace your tracks to Twice Brewed, cross over the Stanegate and the first left will take you to the Roman town and Fort of **Vindolanda** which, apart from archaeological remains, has a good museum with a unique collection of letters preserved in peat, ranging from personal invitations to a birthday party to garrison accounts and reports. The peat has also preserved leather goods and there is a remarkable display of footwear and tunics. The site is still being excavated. Archaeologists give talks on the dig and there are reconstructions of a section of wall, a temple, a shop and a house.

Return to the Stanegate and you will come to **Housesteads** (Vercovium), a fort on the Wall on your left.

Travelling east from here you will see good sections of the Wall on your left and the **Vallum** which is mostly on the right hand side but crosses the road from time to time.

Chesters Fort is on your right just before you join the B6320.

In South Shields, **Arbeia** was the Roman supply base.

All these sites are open all the year round.

For details of opening hours and prices:
www.vindolanda.com,
www.english-heritage.org.uk/hadrianwall
www.twmuseums.org.uk/arbeia

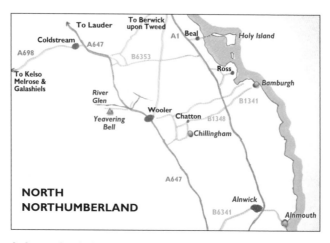

North Northumberland Bryneich

See: 'Post Roman Britain', 'The First Battle' and 'The Last of the Men of the North'

At the end of the Stanegate, follow the signs to Collerton and follow the B6342. This will take you up to Alnwick with its castle and the charming little seaside town of **Alnmouth. See 6th battle.**

The A1 takes you up to **Bamburgh,** site of Dun Guyardi, the capital of Bryneich and reputedly the home of the chief who inspired the legendary Lancelot. A magnificent Norman Keep, the ruins of which were restored in the 19th century, replaced the original Celtic Fort – more impressive from the outside than within.

www.lindisfarne.org.uk, www.bamburghcastle.com

A little further north, you can access the beach and sand dunes at Ross – a landscape which has not changed since the Dark Ages and, looking north west, you can see **Holy Island** with its castle (National Trust – open summer only) and the Priory (English Heritage – open all year) and an exhibition on the Lindisfarne Gospels. The island can be reached at low tide by a causeway from Beal.

Take the B1341 to join the A1 and turn north. Take the first left onto the B6348.

At **Chillingham,** there is a herd of the sacred ancient wild white cattle of Ancient Britain – the only surviving herd of wild cattle in the world. Continue to Wooler and join the A697 north. Open summer only.

www.chillingham-castle.com

For Yeavering Bell and the river Glen, fork left to Akeld on the B63. See 1st battle

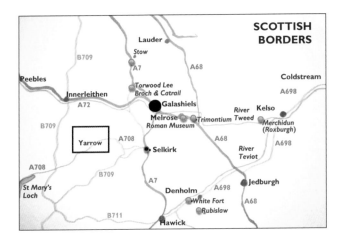

Scottish Borders, East Lothian and Midlothian
Selgovae and Gododdin

See: 'The Roman Legacy', 'Port Roman Britain' and 'The Arthurian Campaign' (7th battle)

To find Ruberslaw, follow the signs to Kirk Yetholm and Jedburgh on the A698 to Denholm (direction Hawick). You will find Ruberslaw just to the south. In Denholm village, turn right uphill. Ignore the first on the left, which leads to a quarry. The second on the left leads up to the farm of Denholm Hill. The farmyard is on your left and the remains of the White Fort are through a wood on your right. **See 8th battle.**

For Yarrow, continue on the A698 to Hawick and turn north on the A7. At Selkirk, go through the town (direction Peebles) to Philiphaugh and turn left on the A708 to Yarrow.

Follow the Yarrow valley crossing over a bridge until you come to a second bridge with a grassy triangle and a single-track road going left over the hills to Etterick. Now follow the map.

The **Warriors Rest** Standing Stone is on your right near the war memorial. It is in the front garden of a cottage but can be seen from the gate.

The **Glebe Stone** is easily visible from the road in the next field, also on your right.

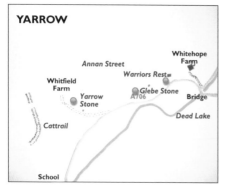

YARROW

Whitehope Farm
Annan Street
Warriors Rest
Whitfield Farm
Yarrow Stone
Glebe Stone
A706
Bridge
Dead Lake
Cattrail
School

The **Yarrow Stone** is up a farm track on the right and surrounded by a wooden railing. The inscription runs sideways down it in six lines of text, so originally the stone must have stood on its long side, with the text readable the right way up, thus marking two graves placed side by side. The two princes would have been in the front rank of the Alt Clut force and the battle was presumably fought principally in the area between the standing stones.

Annan Street is the field to the north where numerous Christian burials were found when the land was first ploughed in 1803.

The flat land in the haugh on the south side of the river opposite the standing stones is **Dead Lake**. On the hillside on your right, you can make out the line of an earthwork – The Catrail (or Picts Work Dyke) – which marked the Selgovian border and which originally came down to cross the river at Yarrow Feus.

Follow the A708 until you come to a cross roads at The Gordon Arms.

Turn right on the B709 to Innerleithen.

In Innerleithen turn left on the A72 to Peebles. Continue down the High St and turn left at the end, staying on the A72. As you come out of Peebles you will pass Neidpath Castle on your left and shortly afterwards there is a turning to the left to Manor Valley. At Kirkton Manor take the left fork and Cademuir Hill is on your left hand side.

Retrace your steps through Peebles and Innerleithen and just before Galashiels park in a lay-by on the A72 and walk down to the entrance gates and lodge of Torwoodlee House. To reach the **Broch**, the access road has a 'Private Road' sign but is a public footpath as far as the waymark on its right hand side. Please respect the owner's privacy beyond this point. At the waymark, turn left on to the woodland path and, in a few yards, you will come to a signpost indicating the path ahead to Torwoodlee Tower and a right turn to the Broch and the remains of the **Catrail.**

In **Melrose** you will find a small **Roman Heritage Museum** in the main square which may help you make more sense of your visit to **Trimontium**. To reach Trimontium, follow the A6091 signed to St Boswells and after a few miles Trimontium is signed to the left.

See: 'The Roman Occupation' and 'The Roman Legacy'
www.trimontium.org.uk

You can then continue on to St Boswells where you turn left on the A699 to Kelso. Just before Kelso, across the river on your left you will see Roxbugh Castle. On your right is the site of the **Merchidun (Roxburgh)** – a heavily overgrown motte where the Teviot joins the Tweed. It is difficult to mount but you can walk along the side of the Teviot where, above you, there are the odd blocks of city wall from Roxburgh which, in the 15th century, was the third major city of Scotland with a

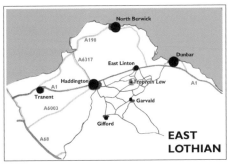

royal mint and a cathedral. In 1460, James II was killed by an exploding canon retaking the town from the English. His widow decided its proximity to the border was a constant cause of trouble and ordered it to be completely demolished.

See: Camelot, Avalon and the Death of Arthur

From Kelso, take the A696 to **Berwick on Tweed**, which was the port for Trimontium and was the boundary of the Gododdin and Bryneich. Later, it became the frontier between England and Scotland and changed hands 14 times.

See: 'The Roman Occupation' and 'The Roman Legacy'
www.visitnorthumberland.co.uk, www.exploreberwick.co.uk

From here, take the A1 north and turn off to Haddington. Go through the main square and straight on following a small road past the golf course. Keep travelling east and you will be able to navigate by eye. You can drive right round **Traprain Law (Dunpender)**, the old Gododdin capital, but access to the summit is by path from a car park in the north side.

See: 'The Roman Legacy' and 'The Druid and the Saint'
www.visiteastlothian.org

The Traprain treasure is on view in the **National Museum of Scotland** in Chambers Street in Edinburgh which, together with the **castle (Dun Eidyn)** and **Arthur's Seat,** should be your next port of call.

See: 'The Roman Occupation', 'The Roman Legacy', 'Camelot, 'Avalon and the Death of Arthur' and 'The Druid and the Saint'
www.nms.ac.uk, www.edinburgh.org

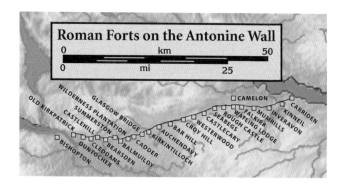

West Lothian and Stirlingshire
The Antonine Wall

See: 'Appendix 1 The Roman occupation', 'The Roman Legacy', 'Arthur and the Enemy' and 'Camelot, Avalon and the Death of Arthur'.

In terms of Roman remains, there is nothing obviously visible at **Camelon** on the site of the Falkirk Gold Club but there is a good section of the wall in Falkirk at **Watling Lodge.** Further west, there are clear sections of the wall and remains of forts at Rough Castle (where the stake pits are clearly visible) and Barr Hill Fort near **Twechar**.
www.historic-scotland.gov.uk/antoninewall

The Antonine Wall runs for 39 miles between the east and west coast. It was built of turf on a stone foundation. The original plan was to build a stone wall similar to Hadrian's Wall, but this was amended to a bank about four metres high with a wide ditch on the north side and a military way on the south. The Romans built forts every two miles (a total of 19). It took 12 years to build (started in 142AD and was held for 20 years before the retreat to Hadrian's Wall). In 208, The Emperor Severus rebuilt it but abandoned it only a few years later.

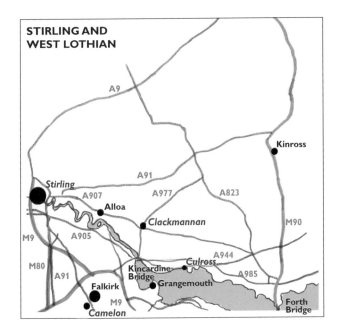

STIRLING AND
WEST LOTHIAN

Stirling, Clackmannan and East Fife
The Manau Gododdin

See: 'The Roman Legacy', 'Arthur and the Enemy' and 'Camelot, Avalon and the Death of Arthur'.

Stirling is reached by the M9 motorway from Edinburgh. You can visit **Stirling Castle, Cambuskenneth Abbey** and find the rampart of the **Dark Age Fort** beside the **Wallace monument** on **Abbey Craig**. A mile and a half to the south is **St Ninians (Eccles)** with its ancient graveyard.
www.stirling.gov.uk/visit, www.visitstirling.org,
www.historic-scotland.gov.uk, www.stirling.gov.uk

Take the A907 to Alloa and **Clackmannan** where you can find the **Mannan Stone** (dating from Pictish times) in the main square before continuing on to **Culross**, an interesting medieval village (National Trust properties open summer only) on the north shore of the Forth beyond Kincardine with its abbey (open all year) where St Mungo was brought up.
www.nts.org.uk/Property/Royal-Burgh-of-Culross

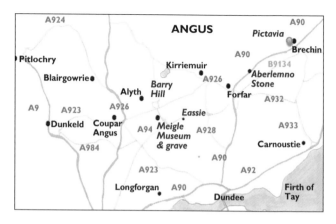

Angus, Perthshire, and Lennox
The Picts

See: 'The Roman Occupation', 'The Roman Legacy', 'The Arthurian Campaign', 'Camelot, Avalon and the Death of Arthur' and 'The Last of the Men of the North'

From Culross, follow the A985 along the north shore of the Forth until it joins the M90 on the north side of the Forth Road Bridge.

Follow the M90 to Perth and then take the A94 to Coupar Angus and Meigle (direction Forfar). At **Meigle,** visit the Museum of carved Pictish Stones. In the churchyard is **Vanora's Mound** and, close by, **Barry Hill** – the hillfort to which Guinevere (Vanora) was supposedly abducted or fled.

Continue on the A94. You could detour a few miles south to **Eassie** where there is another interesting stone in the ruined church.

At **Glamis,** in the Manse garden, is a Pictish cross slab and there are other fragments inside the church itself.

At **Forfar,** the Meffan Museum and Art Gallery in West High St houses a fine collection of sculptured stones.

At Forfar take the B9134 to Brechin. At **Aberlemno,** you will pass the stone which depicts the final victory of the Picts over the Angles at Nechtestan. At Brechin, turn left and visit **Pictavia,** an interpretation centre which tells the story of the Picts.

www.angusahead.com/visit, www.angusanddundee.co.uk
www.pictavia.org.uk, www.historic-scotland.gov.uk

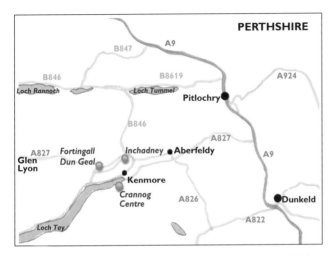

From Brechin, return via the A90 and B957 to Kirriemuir, the A926 to Blairgowrie and the A923 to Dunkeld.

Turn up the A9 and turn off at Logierait. Take the A827 to Aberfeldy (where you can make a detour to **Fortingall** which has the oldest tree in Europe in the graveyard – a 3,000 year old yew). The White Fort on the hill above is on a private estate. **See 8th battle**. It is difficult to find and pretty inaccessible.
www.undiscoveredscotland.co.uk/fortingall/fortingall/index.html

From Aberfeldy, carry on to Kenmore and on the south side of the loch visit **the Crannog Centre** (a lake dwelling), which replicates the Iron Age but would have been pretty similar in the Dark Ages.
www.crannog.co.uk

The well at **Inchadney** is in the grounds of Taymouth Castle, below **The Gallops**. To find it, go through Kenmore, cross the bridge over the Tay and take the first right.

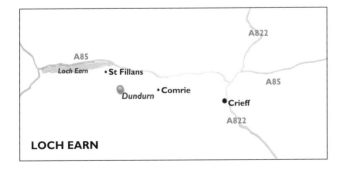

Return to Aberfeldy and take the A826 and A822 to Crieff. Then follow the A85 through Comrie and **the Pictish fort** at **Dundurn** is on your left a mile or so before you reach St Fillans on Loch Earn. **See 7th battle.**

Keep on the A85 to Crianlarich and take the A82 to Tarbet and Loch Lomond. Look out for the **Falls of Falloch** on your left. This was the Pictish frontier with Alt Clut. The **Clach nam Breatan** is 2,000 feet higher up the mountain. It cannot be seen from the road, there is no path and it is a climb of about two miles over a peat bog.

The territorial limits of Dalriada are also marked about 10km to the south, above Lochgoilhead by a boulder known as Clach nam Breatunnaich and 24km west, near the coast at Morvern, by another artificial hummock. On a line between the three are place names incorporating 'Criche' or 'Fala', meaning boundary.

The first river crossing the road is the **Alt Fionn Ghleann**. See 1st battle.

The next river round a corner, where the ground begins to widen, is the **Dubh Eas**. **Glen Douglas** is the first glen going south from Tarbet. **See 2nd battle.**

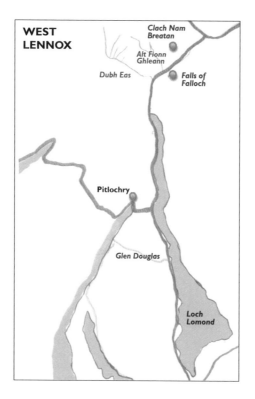

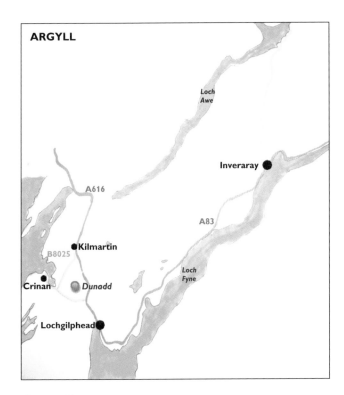

ARGYLL

Loch Awe

Inveraray ●

A616

A83

● Kilmartin

B8025

Crinan ●   ◯ Dunadd

Loch Fyne

Lochgilphead ●

Argyll
The Scots

See: 'The Roman Legacy', 'The Arthurian Campaign' and 'The Last of the Men of the North'

From Tarbet take the A83 to **Arrochar** (home of Caw) and, with Ben Arthur on your right, climb the long haul up Rest And Be Thankful. Driving along the north side of Loch Fyne, pass Inveraray to Lochgilphead.

At Lochgilphead, take the A616 north and, just after you pass the turning to the Crinan Canal and a couple of miles before Kilmartin, you will find **Dunadd**, the capital of Dalriada, on the left hand side of the road. It is signed on the right hand side of the road but the sign is fairly small and easy to miss. A single-track road will take you there. It is well maintained and there is a car park.

See: 'The Roman Legacy', 'The Arthurian Campaign'.

The site has been excavated by archaeologists on three occasions and, as a result, a fair amount is known about it. It originally had four lines of walls at different levels.

A rocky defile, even without the walls that would once have added to it, marks the entrance and ascends through the lower terraces. At the summit, you can find a partial stretch of original wall. Just below the summit is a bowl carved out of the rock which one can guess perhaps played a part in an anointing or purification ritual. Two footprints also carved into the rock suggest that, following Irish tradition, the High Chief of Dalriada was inaugurated by setting his foot into the imprint of his forbears. There is also a seat in the rock. Was this a throne and is this where the Stone of Destiny was kept? A High Chief was elected but had to be the son and the grandson of a High Chief. He was confirmed by popular vote and, in the case of disaster, could be impeached by the people and replaced.

www.darkisle.com/d/dunadd/dunadd.html

A little further on is the **Kilmartin Archaeological Museum**, which explains the 150 prehistoric sites in the Glen (burial chambers, standing stones and stone circles).

www.kilmartin.org

By **Crinan** is the beach where the boats arrived from Antrim and there is a small museum about the canal.

Dumbarton
Alt Clut

See: 'The Roman Occupation', 'The Roman
Legacy', 'The Arthurian Campaign, 'The Last
of the Men of the North'

Retrace your steps to Arrochar and take the
A814 on the south side of Loch Long. The
first road to the left will take you through
Glen Douglas, southern boundary of the
northernmost sub-chiefdom of the Alt Clut.

See 2nd battle

At Loch Lomond turn south on the A82 to
Dumbarton. Go into the town centre and
follow the directions to **Dumbarton Castle**
on the rock which was the capital of the Alt Clut.
(Historic Scotland – open all year).
www.historic-Scotland.gov.uk
www.undiscoveredscotland.co.uk/
dumbartoncastle

Head for Glasgow on the A82, cross the Clyde via the Erskine Bridge. In
Govan Old Parish Church, there is a fine collection of sculptured stones

In **Glasgow,** the **Cathedral** was founded by St Mungo. The Glasgow coat of
arms shows the fish with a ring held in its mouth. The story goes that the High
Chief of Alt Clut had given his wife a ring as a present. But the Chief's wife
gave it to a courtier who promptly lost it. Some versions of the story say that
the Chief took the ring while the courtier was asleep and threw it in the river.
The Chief then demanded to see the ring – threatening death to this wife if
she could not do so. The courtier confessed to St Mungo who sent a monk
to catch a fish in the river Clyde. When this was brought back St Mungo cut
open the fish and found the ring.

Upper Tweedale and Dumfries Merlin

See: 'The Druid and the Saint'

Biggar

A72

Alter Stane

A703

River Tweed Peebles

Broughton •

B712

Stobo

A702

A701

•Tinnis Castle
Drumelzier

River Tweed

St Mary's Loch

Hart Fell

•Ericstane
Auchencat
Burn

A708

M6

Moffat

**UPPER TWEEDALE
AND DUMFRIESSHIRE**

Take the M8 motorway in the direction of Edinburgh. This takes you through the centre of Glasgow so avoid rush hour. Exit at junction six towards Lanark on the A73 through Newmains, Carluke, Lanark. After Thankerton, branch right to Symington on the A72. At Biggar, turn off to Broughton. At Broughton, go south on the A701 and turn right on the B712 to **Drumelzier.**

As you come out of Drumelzier, there is a small humpback bridge. On the left hand side there is a track which follows the burn and bends left to join the Tweed. Follow this and, where the burn meets the river, go through a small gate and, immediately on your right hand side, there is a thorn bush. Enclosed in a fence is small metal sign, half hidden in the undergrowth, identifying the spot where Merlin met his triple death.

Continue on the B712 towards Peebles. The road crosses the Tweed just after Bellspool. Take the first left and make a U-turn on to a narrow road. Follow this until you come to a farm on the left hand side. Opposite the entrance to the farm in a wood, the **Alter Stane** where Merlin was baptised is at the side of the road. Travel back to the B712 and continue towards Peebles until you come to **Stobo Kirk,** which is well worth a visit and is the site where Merlin met St Mungo.

From Stobo, follow the B712 until it joins the A72 at Lyne Station. To find Lyne Roman Fort, turn right to Hallyne (half a mile) or turn right to Peebles. Go through Peebles to Innerleithen and turn off on the B709, which goes through Traquair to Mount Benger (Gordon Arms) where you join the A708. Turn right to Moffat and go past St Mary's Loch on your left and further on to the Grey Mare's Tail waterfall.

At Moffat, turn north up the High Street but as you exit the town do not follow the A701 but follow the small road to Ericstane. This road is a dead end.

About half a mile before Ericstane you will find a green community hall on your right and a stile with a signpost to **Hartfell**. If you follow the track you will see a scar of scree on Hart Fell. Follow the burn up into the cleugh. This is where you will find the chalybeate spring and Merlin's hiding place.

From Moffat, join the M74 south. At Gretna Green turn off to Longtown and, at the end of the main street, there is turn off to the right to **Arthuret Church** which is on the site of the chapel overlooking the river, built to commemorate the victory of Christianity over paganism where the slaughter sent Merlin mad.

www.visitcumbria.com

Return to Gretna and follow the A75 to Dumfries, Castle Douglas and Newton Stewart.

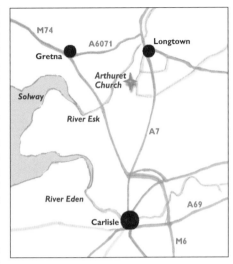

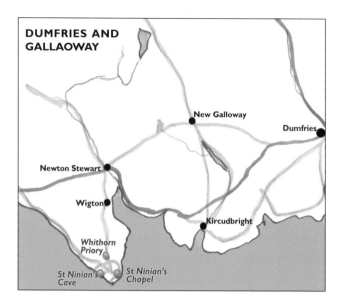

Galloway

St Ninian

See: 'Arthur of the Britons' and 'The Arthurian Campaign'

From Newton Stewart, take the A714 to Wigton which continues as the A746 to Whithorn.

The outline of **St Ninian's Church (Candida Casa)** can be seen in the graveyard alongside the ruins of the medieval priory in Whithorn itself.

St Ninian's Cave is on the west side of Burrow head, at the western end of the Solway.

At the Isle of Whithorn, there is **St Ninian's Chapel** and the small beach where pilgrims came ashore. Car parking is easy at all the sites and access is not difficult.

www.whithorn.info, www.whithorn.com

Follow the A714 north to Girvan and take the A77 north to Ayr.

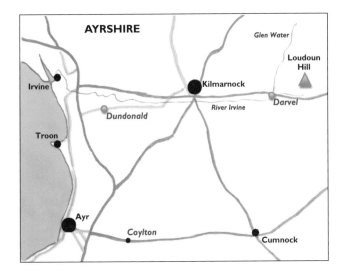

Ayrshire

Aeron

See: The First Battle

The **Water of Coyle,** where Old King Coel met his end in a peat bog, is crossed by the B736 which runs from just north of Polnessan on the A70 from Ayr to Cumnock.

Continue north on the A77 and, at Troon, turn right on the A759 to Kilmarnock. At the first crossroads turn off for the fort at **Dundonald** which is now the site of a medieval castle (open in the summer only).
www.dundonaldcastle.org.uk

Continue on the A759 to join the A71 at Kilmarnock and head east to **Darvel**. The mouth of the **River Glen** can be found following a footpath through a small housing estate in Darvel. **Loudoun Hill** is slightly further east on the A71 in the direction of Strathaven. Continue on to join the M74.

Your Arthurian circuit in Scotland is now complete.

Going south via **Carlisle,** a visit to the **castle** and **Tullie House Museum** is of interest.

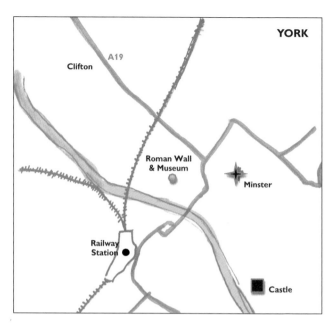

England
York

See: 'Appendix 1 The Roman Occupation', 'The Roman Legacy' and the
9th and 19th battles

Enter York on the A19 from Easingwold and Thirsk. In the centre of town, turn
right down Marygate and walk into the museum gardens. The **Roman tower**
and a section of the **Roman wall** is just beyond the **museum building.**
www.visityork.org

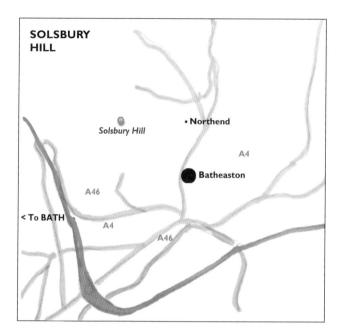

SOLSBURY
HILL

Solsbury Hill

• Northend

A4

● Batheaston

A46

< To BATH

A4

A46

Bath

Little Solsbury Hill

See: 12th battle

Turn off the M4 at junction 18 and follow the A46 to where it bends just outside Bath at a roundabout. Turn left to Batheaston on the A4. In Batheaston, turn left to Northend and the first on the left is Solsbury Lane. This is single track with few passing places. Near the top, fork right. This will bring you to the fort at the top of the hill but there is no parking

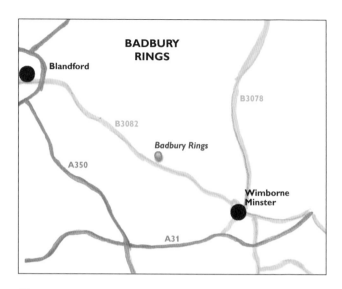

Dorset

Badbury Rings

See: 12th battle

Badbury Rings are on the B3062 on the right hand side of the road between Wimborne Minster and Blandford. Parking and easy access.

See 12th battle.
www.nationaltrust.org.uk/main/w-vh/.../w-kingstonlacy-estate.htm

To Follow the Legend

In England

www.legendofkingarthur.co.uk/southern-england-king-arthur.htm
en.wikipedia.org/wiki/Monmouth_Priory;
www.english-heritage.org.uk/daysout/properties/tintagel-castle;
www.arthur-online.co.uk/

In Wales

www.legendofkingarthur.co.uk/wales-king-arthur.htm

In France

www.centre-arthurien-broceliande.com/menu.html
en.wikipedia.org/wiki/Avallon

Bibliography

I would like to credit the work of previous authors, particularly:

Alcock, Leslie. 1998. *Arthur's Britain – History and Archaeology*. Penguin

Ashe, Geoffrey. 1968. *The Quest for Arthur's Britain*. Pall Mall Press, London

Bartrum. Peter C. 1993. *A Welsh Classical Dictionary*.

Bede, The Venerable. 1903. *Ecclesiastical History of the English Nation*. JM Dent & Sons, London

Bowie. W. 1855. *The Black Book of Taymouth*, Bannatyne Club, Edinburgh

Bromwich, R. 1963. *Scotland and the earliest Arthurian tradition*. Bibliog. Bull. Int. Arthurian Soc.

Chadwick, Nora. 1971. *The Celts*. Pelican Books, London

Clarkson, Tim. 2008. *The Picts, A History*. Birlinn, Edinburgh

Composite 1980. *The Problem of the Picts*. Melven Press

Dodds, Ross Mackenzie. 2010 *Aberfeldy and the History of a Highland Community* Watermill Books

Elliot, Walter. 2010. *Selkirkshire and the Borders*. Deerpark Press

Fraser, James. E. 2009. *From Caledonia to Pictland*. Edinburgh University Press

Goodrich, N.L. 1986. *King Arthur*. Harper and Row, New York

Glennie, J.S.S. 1988. *An Arthurian Reader*. Matthews, J., ed. Oxford University Press

Glennie J.S.S 1994 *Arthurian Localities in Scotland*, Llanerch, Felinfach

Ingram. Rev. James translation. 1912. *The Anglo Saxon Chronicle* JM Dent & Sons, London

Jackson, Arthur. 1984. *The Symbol Stones of Scotland*. Orkney Press

Konstam. Angus. 2010. *Stronghholds of the Picts*. Osprey Publishing

Lowe, Chris. 1999. *Angles, Fools and Tyrants*. Canongate

Moffat, Alistair. 1999. *Arthur and the Lost Kingdoms*, Wiedenfield & Nicolson

McHardy, Stuart. 2003. *The Quest for Arthur*, Luath Press, Edinburgh

McHardy, Stuart 2003 *The Quest for the Nine Maidens*, Edinburgh, Luath Press

Ritchie, Anna. 1999. *Picts*. Historic Scotland

Ross, David. 2001. *Scottish Place Names*. Birlinn, Edinburgh

Skene, W.H. 1876. *Celtic Scotland: A History of Ancient Alban*. Vol. I, *History and Ethnology*. Edmonston and Douglas, Edinburgh

Smith, William & Wace, Henry. 1877. *The Dictionary of Christian Biography*.

Smyth, Alfred.P. 1984. *Warlords and Holymen, Scotland AD80 – 1000*. Edinburgh University Press

Thomas, Charles. *The Interpretation of the Pictish Symbols.* Archaeological Journal Vol CXX

Wagner, Paul. 2002, *Pictish Warrior AD 297–241.* Osprey Publishing

Acknowledgements

I also thank the members of l'association Charles Rennie Mackintosh en Roussillon, and archaeologist Tarek Kuteni who prompted me during a visit to Scotland in 2009 to embark on this project. Also archaeologist Stephen Digney for valuable criticism and corrections.

I also thank Campbell Chesterman, Sylvia Woodcock Clark, Sir Robert Clerk, Murray Cook, Louise Crichton, Flora Crichton, Miglet Crichton, Jean Michel Gontier (Tandem), Donald Gordon, Norman and Maggie Hacket, John Blair Keddie, Lynda McGuigan, Stephanie Wolfe Murray, Hannah Buchanan Smith, Robewert Kenny Smith, Linda Sinclair, Cara Roberts, Arno Vilanove and the staff of the Roman Army Museum in Melrose, Pictavia in Brechin and Vindolanda on Hadrian's Wall.

Monsieur Mackintosh:
Charles Rennie Mackintosh
in Roussillon
Robin Crichton
ISBN 978-1-905222-36-0 PBK £15.00

In 1923 Charles and Margaret
Mackintosh escaped Britain for
France. *Monsieur Mackintosh* is the
only book available on Mackintosh's
years in France. With reproductions
of 40 of his French paintings
alongside photographs of the
actual locations today, and images
from the period 1923–1927, this
is a comprehensive and pictorial
account.

Written in close collaboration with
experts from Glasgow University,
the National Gallery of Modern
Art and the Glasgow School of Art,
and edited by Professor Pamela
Robertson, author and leading
expert on Mackintosh, *Monsieur
Mackintosh* includes new research
and is written with the French
and English translations side-
by-side. Published to coincide
with and accompany a major
exhibition of Mackintosh's work in
France *Monsieur Mackintosh* contains
more than 250 images reproduced in
full colour throughout.

*… [A] beautifully illustrated book…
Crichton's bilingual French–English text
draws on Mackintosh's own letters and
journals to offer some touching insights
into the restorative capacities of both
travel and art.*
THE SCOTSMAN

The Quest for Arthur

Stuart McHardy

ISBN 978-1-842820-12-4 HBK £16.99

King Arthur of Camelot and the Knights of the Round Table are enduring romantic figures. A national hero for the Britons, the Welsh and the English alike, Arthur is a potent figure for many.

Historian, storyteller and folklorist Stuart McHardy believes he has uncovered the origins of the true Arthur. He incorporates knowledge of folklore and place-name studies with an archaeological understanding of the sixth century.

This quest leads to the discovery that the enigmatic origins of Arthur lie not in Brittany, England or Wales. Instead they lie in that magic land the ancient Welsh called Y Gogledd, 'The North', the North of Britain, which we now call – Scotland.

[Stuart McHardy's] findings are set to shake established Arthurian thinking.
THE SCOTSMAN

On the Trail of the Holy Grail

Stuart McHardy

ISBN 978-1-905222-53-7 PBK £7.99

New theories appear and old ideas are re-configured as this remarkable story continues to fascinate and enthral.

Scholars have long known that the Grail is essentially legendary, a mystic symbol forever sought by those seeking Enlightenment, a quest in which the search is as important as the result. Time and again it has been said that the Grail is a construct of mystical Christian ideas and motifs from the ancient oral tradition of the Celtic-speaking peoples of Britain. There is much to commend this view, but now, drawing on decades of research in his native Scotland, in a major new contribution to the Grail legend, the field historian and folklorist Stuart McHardy traces the origin of the idea of fertility and regeneration back beyond the time of the Celtic warrior tribes of Britain to a truly ancient, physical source.

A physical source as dynamic and awesome today as it was in prehistory when humans first encountered it and began to weave the myths that grew into the Legend of the Holy Grail.

… a refreshingly different approach to the origin of the Grail.
NOTHERN EARTH

Luath Press Limited
committed to publishing well written books worth reading

LUATH PRESS takes its name from Robert Burns, whose little collie Luath (*Gael.*, swift or nimble) tripped up Jean Armour at a wedding and gave him the chance to speak to the woman who was to be his wife and the abiding love of his life. Burns called one of 'The Twa Dogs' Luath after Cuchullin's hunting dog in Ossian's *Fingal*. Luath Press was established in 1981 in the heart of Burns country, and now resides a few steps up the road from Burns' first lodgings on Edinburgh's Royal Mile.
Luath offers you distinctive writing with a hint of unexpected pleasures.

Most bookshops in the UK, the US, Canada, Australia, New Zealand and parts of Europe either carry our books in stock or can order them for you. To order direct from us, please send a £sterling cheque, postal order, international money order or your credit card details (number, address of cardholder and expiry date) to us at the address below. Please add post and packing as follows: UK – £1.00 per delivery address; overseas surface mail – £2.50 per delivery address; overseas airmail – £3.50 for the first book to each delivery address, plus £1.00 for each additional book by airmail to the same address. If your order is a gift, we will happily enclose your card or message at no extra charge.

Luath Press Limited
543/2 Castlehill
The Royal Mile
Edinburgh EH1 2ND
Scotland
Telephone: 0131 225 4326 (24 hours)
Fax: 0131 225 4324
email: sales@luath.co.uk
Website: www.luath.co.uk